CONTE

When the Chief Shepherd appears,
you will receive the crown of glory that does not fade away...
To Him be the glory and dominion forever and ever.

Amen.

1 PETER 5:4,11

ED HINDSON

FUTURE GLORY

HARVEST PROPHECY
AN IMPRINT OF HARVEST HOUSE PUBLISHERS

Special thanks to Dillon Burroughs and Daniel Sloan for their editorial assistance.

Cover design by Bryce Williamson

Cover photo © AlexSava, BessHamiti / Gettyimages

Interior design by Aesthetic Soup

For bulk, special sales, or ministry purchases, please call 1-800-547-8979.
Email: Customerservice@hhpbooks.com

is a trademark of the Hawkins Children's LLC. Harvest House Publishers, Inc., is the exclusive licensee of the trademark .

Future Glory
Copyright © 2021 by Ed Hindson
Published by Harvest House Publishers
Eugene, Oregon 97408
www.harvesthousepublishers.com

ISBN 978-0-7369-8350-1 (pbk.)
ISBN 978-0-7369-8351-8 (eBook)

Library of Congress Cataloging-in-Publication Data

Names: Hindson, Edward E., author.
Title: Future glory : living in the hope of the rapture, heaven, and
  eternity / Ed Hindson.
Description: Eugene, Oregon : Harvest House Publishers, [2021] | Summary:

Identifiers: LCCN 2020050001 (print) | LCCN 2020050002 (ebook) | ISBN
  9780736983501 (pbk) | ISBN 9780736983518 (ebook)
Subjects: LCSH: Future life—Christianity. | Eternity.
Classification: LCC BT903 .H56 2021 (print) | LCC BT903 (ebook) | DDC
  236/.24—dc23
LC record available at https://lccn.loc.gov/2020050001
LC ebook record available at https://lccn.loc.gov/2020050002

Printed in the United States of America

21 22 23 24 25 26 27 28 29 / BP / 10 9 8 7 6 5 4

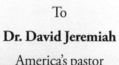

To

Dr. David Jeremiah

America's pastor

Bible expositor

prophetic preacher

and

lifelong friend

PREFACE

God has planned an incredible eternal experience for every believer. We were created for eternity and redeemed for eternity. But life has a way of focusing our attention on our immediate cares and not our ultimate goal. We are easily caught up in our daily tasks that take most of our time and attention away from the ultimate purpose for which we were created. The Bible reminds us that while God has "made everything beautiful in its time," He has also "put eternity in [our] hearts" (Ecclesiastes 3:11). No matter how hard we try, we are never satisfied with anything less than that which is eternal. Joe Stowell said, "Life is most disappointing, most despairing when it is lived as though this world is all we have."[1]

Jesus said of those who believed in Him, "And I give them eternal life, and they shall never perish" (John 10:28). As He prayed the night before His crucifixion, Jesus said, "And this is eternal life, that they may know You, the only true God, and Jesus Christ whom You have sent" (John 17:3). In his first letter, Jesus' disciple John said, "These things I have written to you who believe in the name of the Son of God, that you may know that you have eternal life (1 John 5:13).

Eternity is a long time. It lasts forever. Sometimes people ask: What will we be doing all that time? They assume once we die and go to heaven that's all there is to your eternal life. But the Bible promises so much more. In fact, there are at least seven things predicted in Scripture that every believer will eventually experience. In the pages that follow, we will examine those seven promises and all that they will mean in your amazing future.

Once we understand the sequence of events that God has planned for our eternal future, we can face the future with confidence. If we can trust Him for heaven, we can trust Him for eternity. The last thing we will be doing is floating around alone on a cloud. In the vast expanse of the universe, we will serve the Lord forever. We will be busy, active, and living in a redeemed community in perfect fellowship with the entire family of God.

In recent years, I have had the wonderful privilege of speaking about our eternal destiny to vast audiences of believers in some of America's greatest churches. Once people grasp all that God has planned for their eternal future, they are thrilled, blessed, and amazed beyond all their expectations. In the pages that follow, I want to take you with me on an incredible journey into our prophetic future and our eternal destiny.

1

DOES GOD REALLY HAVE A FUTURE FOR ME?

God has planned an amazing future for every believer. What we have already experienced of God's grace in our lives is just a glimpse of all that He has prepared for us. We have more living ahead of us than behind us. We have only just begun our eternal journey. The Bible reminds us:

> "Eye has not seen, nor ear heard...
> The things which God has prepared for those who love
> Him."
>
> (1 Corinthians 2:9)

I have been in the ministry for over fifty years, trying to help people go to heaven. While I've discovered most people want to go to heaven, they are not in a hurry to get there. Most of us go out of our way to delay the inevitable. If the destination is so great, why do we go kicking and screaming? If heaven is real, then we should have a driving passion to be there. We don't want to rush the timing of God, but neither should we dread all that the Lord has for us.

There is a joke told about a married couple in their fifties. They were in terrible health and ate all the wrong things. Finally, the wife became convicted of their ways and told her husband, "We have to start a really serious diet or we're not going to live much longer."

She put him on a strict diet of water, kale, bananas, and not much more! Sure enough, they lost weight and looked great. About ten years later they were tragically killed in a car accident. As they arrived in heaven, they discovered it was more phenomenal than they could have ever imagined. Heaven was more beautiful than they had ever dreamed. There was food everywhere! You could eat all you wanted and never gain weight. There were golf courses and swimming pools. It was unbelievable.

The wife looked at her husband and said, "Isn't this wonderful?"

He looked at her and answered, "Yes! And if it wasn't for you and that awful health food, we could have been here ten years ago!"

I want to remind you, we are on a journey. Our journey has a destination. That destination is heaven. The older you get the more clearly you realize that this world is not all there is in your future.

The older you are, the sooner you want Jesus to come back. Why? Because you're running out of time! On the other hand, my students at university are in no hurry for Him to come. They say things like, "I hope Jesus isn't going to come too soon!"

"Why?"

"I'm not married! I don't want Him to come before I get married." Then six months after they're married they want to know, "How soon is He coming?"

I like to remind them that a God who loves them enough to send His Son to the cross to die for their sins, loves them enough to come back when the time is right. You can trust Him for His perfect timing. The promises in Scripture are very clear that whoever has the Son has eternal life (1 John 5:12). Once you receive Jesus as your Savior, the Spirit of God comes to live within your heart and soul. You already have eternal life. Believers will simply change the place of our existence with that gift of everlasting life. We will live forever because the eternal God lives in us.

The Bible describes God as "the One who is high and lifted up, who inhabits eternity" and yet, dwells "with him who is of a contrite and lowly spirit" (Isaiah 57:15 esv). Think of it! The almighty, eternal God has made us eternally alive by the power of His Spirit and the presence of His person (Romans 8:11). We shall live as long as God lives because He lives in us.

I grew up in a non-Christian home. There was no God, no Jesus, no Bible—nobody attended church. My parents were not raging atheists of any sort. They simply didn't know any better and didn't really care. They were just trying to do the best they could. Both of my parents dropped out of school in the eighth grade. They had to survive the Depression and World War II. They worked their entire lives but with what appeared to be no real meaning or purpose. Certainly with no eternal perspective.

Then one day, a flier came to our home from a local church that was advertising Vacation Bible School. My mother read the flyer and it said the activity lasted five days. She probably thought, *I can get him out of the house for five days!* It was at that event, VBS, I heard that Jesus loved me, that He died for my sins, that He rose from the dead, and that He could give me the gift of everlasting life. Salvation was free, and even in my young mind I recognized a good deal. I raised my hand, "Yes, I'm in! I'm ready to agree to that."

I'm thankful that the lady who counseled me, Mrs. Johnson, was very thorough in helping me understand this was not just a little kid decision about Santa Claus. This was the real deal for the rest of my life. "Are you willing to commit your life to Jesus Christ as Lord and Savior?" she asked. "Are you ready to say yes to Him?"

God moved in my heart for me to say, "Yes, I'm ready for that. I believe. I'll trust Him as my Savior right now."

I realize not every childhood profession is the real thing, but for me it was the real deal. It was a change of course for me and ultimately for our family. I returned home that last day of Vacation Bible School and my mother asked, "How was Bible school today?"

"It was great! I got saved," I said exuberantly.

She had no idea what I was talking about. She patted me on the head and said, "That's nice. What did you make?"

"It's not about the stuff we made, it's about giving my life to Jesus. I've come to know Him as my Savior forever!"

My parents eventually did come to faith in their forties and had a lot of catching up to do. Yet God began to change the course of our entire family experience at that point, just as He has changed many others over the centuries.

So much has taken place in my life since that time. We now live in a world where we have an overabundance of news—and most of it is bad. Even when people talk about Bible prophecy, the focus is often on doom and gloom. To be sure, there are divine judgments that will take place in the future. I do not want to overlook the seriousness of those future judgments.

Serious Bible readers have long understood the dual principles of good news for believers and bad news for unbelievers. Believers understand that God is in control of the details of our lives. Whether we live or die, heaven is our destiny. Therefore, we live with confidence in the future because we know who holds the future.

At the same time, our hearts go out to unbelievers who face eternity without God. Many will be left behind in a world under the judgment of the wrath of God. The recent crisis of the global pandemic is but a glimpse of a far greater disaster that awaits the unbelieving world in the future (Revelation 6:8).

However, in this book, I want to talk about the positive aspects we can look forward to regarding the last days. As believers, we need hope. I don't need to remind you we are facing some of the most precarious times in the history of the world. The future of our nation and the whole world is really at stake. We can focus on the problems, but sometimes if we focus too much on the negative, we lose sight of our real destiny.

I'm reminded of the words of the apostle John who said, "Beloved, now we are children of God; and it has not yet been revealed what we shall be, but we know that when He is revealed, we shall be like Him, for we shall see Him as He is. And everyone who has this hope in Him purifies himself, just as He is pure" (1 John 3:2-3). There is something about the hope of the coming of Christ that lifts us up for the challenges of life here today.

Jesus appeared to John on the island of Patmos. John was one of the original disciples. He was the one who sat next to Jesus at the Last Supper. He was the only disciple who showed up at the cross. John was the one to whom Jesus entrusted the earthly care of His mother. Yet when John saw the glorified Jesus, he said, "When I saw Him, I fell at His feet as dead" (Revelation 1:17).

Don't think it will be a casual thing to wander into heaven and say, "Hi. Where's Jesus?" If John fell on his face, where do you think we will be? On our faces worshipping the Savior, the King of kings and the Lord of lords. The one who loved us, died for us, and gave Himself for us. Because we believe He literally rose from the dead, the promise is that we will also literally live with Him forever.

We're living in a time when people don't understand the literal parts of the Bible. I've had people ask me, "Well, if you die and go to heaven as a spirit, isn't that good enough?" No, because the promise of the Bible is that your body will literally be resurrected one day and reunited with your spirit at the time of the rapture. The Lord will bring with Him those that have departed, raise the dead bodies, rapture the living, and we will all be caught up together to meet the Lord in the air (1 Thessalonians 4:13-17).

In Bible prophecy, the main things are the plain things. The facts are clear. Jesus said, "If I go and prepare a place for you, I will come again and receive you to Myself; that where I am, there you may be also" (John 14:1-3). He will receive us to Himself. Jesus said this after Judas, the unbeliever, left the room. That promise was not only for the eleven believing disciples; it is a promise for every believer of all time. God has promised that Christ will return for us.

I have found the following paradigm to be helpful when interpreting biblical prophecies:

Fact: Jesus is coming again.

Interpretation: When and how (views)

Speculation: How old will we be in heaven?

In this chapter, we will preview the seven amazing ***promises*** we can look forward to in eternity as believers in Jesus Christ. We'll talk more about each of these in the chapters to follow. For now, let me briefly introduce each of these seven promises and why they are important.

1. The Rapture of Believers

The next major event on the prophetic calendar is the rapture of the church. There are a lot of things that *might* happen before the rapture occurs. But there is nothing that *must* happen before the archangel shouts, the trumpet sounds, and we leave this world to be with Christ.

The belief in the rapture is a fundamental truth of biblical theology. Yet so many people today are abandoning belief in the rapture. I was sitting in a church where a friend of mine from another denomination was the pastor. He was preaching an entire sermon *against* the rapture. After about fifty minutes, he said, "And so we see there never will be a rapture. All we have to look forward to is trouble, trouble, and more trouble."

As he ended the sermon, his own congregation moaned out loud. I was tempted to stand up in the back and shout, "Therefore comfort one another with these words" (from 1 Thessalonians 4:18), but I didn't. Instead, I talked to him after the service. I said, "I know you and I have a different view on the timing of the rapture. But we both know there must be a rapture. There has to be a time when the dead are raised and the living are caught up. We just differ on *when* it's going to happen."

If you disagree on the timing of the rapture, please don't tell people, "There's never going to be a rapture." No, there must be a rapture or the Bible is not true. There must be a time when the archangel shouts, when the trumpet sounds, and the dead in Christ are raised and the living are caught up (1 Thessalonians 4:13-18). We may differ on *timing* of the rapture but not the *fact* of the rapture.

You may hear people say, "The word *rapture* is not in the Bible. Why should I believe in the rapture if it's not in the Bible?" Well, the word *Bible* is not in the Bible. But the concept of inspired Scripture is (2 Timothy 3:16). The word for rapture in the original Greek New Testament is the word *harpazo,* meaning to be "caught up" or "snatched away." The word *Trinity* is not in the Bible either, but we believe in the triune God, the co-equal deity of Father, Son, and Holy Spirit. The word is not in the Bible, but the concept is. The word *Sunday* is not in the Bible, but we worship on Sunday as the Lord's Day because that's when Jesus rose from the dead and the early church assembled to celebrate the risen Lord on that day. A concept can be taught in Scripture whether the word appears there in English or not.

The truth of the Bible is there *must* be a rapture. There must be a catching up. There must be a time when dead believers are raised, and the living are caught up into the presence of God. If somebody doesn't believe in the pretribulational rapture, they should not go around saying, "Well, I don't believe there is ever going to be a rapture." They simply don't agree with the *timing* of the event. The fact of the rapture is clear in the Bible. If you say you don't believe in the rapture, you don't believe the Bible. You might as well rip 1 Thessalonians 4 out of the Bible and throw it away. It's the whole basis of the believer's blessed hope (Titus 2:13).

I've even heard some critics teach, "I don't think all those things about the future are really essential doctrines." Did you know the apostle Paul was in Thessalonica for only about three weeks (Acts 17:1-10)? During that time, he taught them about the second coming of Christ (2 Thessalonians 2:5). Apparently, he considered it an essential doctrine.

Suppose someone said to you, "I'm going away on a long trip. I'm going to be gone for a long time, but I will be back." If that was someone you loved with all your heart, you'd be watching for them to return. This promise was not made by a human being. It was made by the Son of God (Matthew 25:14-19). He will come back for you. The first amazing promise we have to look forward to as believers in Christ is the rapture of the living and the resurrection of the dead.

2. The Father's House

Second, *where* do we go at the time of the rapture? We are going to the Father's house. Why? Because Jesus promised to take the bride home to the Father's house. In John 14, Jesus taught that in His Father's house are many rooms. The King James Version says "mansions" and has given people the idea we'll each have our own luxury estate. However, the original language mentions "rooms." Why? Because it is one big house, with lots of rooms. All the believers of all time are going to dwell together in the Father's mansion.

Jesus taught in John 14:3-4, "And if I go and prepare a place for you, I will come again and receive you to Myself; that where I am, there you may be also. And where I go you know, and the way you know." The rapture must occur at some point prior to this to take the bride to the Father's house. This heaven will also clearly be a physical place. Ron Rhodes explains:

> There are numerous indications in the New Testament that heaven will be a physical place. For example, as noted previously in this book, Jesus in John 14:1-3 affirmed: "In my Father's *house* are many *rooms*; if it were not so, I would have told you. I am going there to prepare *a place* for you. And if I go and prepare a place for you, I will come back and take you to be with me that you also may be where I am" (emphasis added). The words "house," "rooms," and "a place" suggest a physical place where the physically resurrected redeemed will forever live.[1]

Now people can argue on the details of the timing. They can say they think the rapture is before the tribulation, or in the middle, or at the end, but it must happen somewhere. You can't just throw it away. You must place it somewhere. Ask yourself, "What are the factors in the timing?"

At some point, the Lord will come in the clouds, resurrect the dead, rapture the living, and take the bride to the Father's house—to heaven! He's been preparing that place for almost two thousand years. If He could create the world instantly and it's as beautiful as it is even under the curse of sin, imagine what heaven will look like. He's been working on it all this time ever since He left. When the Father says, "Go get the bride and bring her to the Father's house," then Jesus will come for His own. Every genuine believer since the first day Jesus gave that promise until the rapture of the entire bride of Christ will be gathered together to the Father's house.

3. The Judgment Seat of Christ

Third, we go to the Father's house to the judgment seat of Christ. Paul said in 2 Corinthians 5:10, "We must all appear before the judgment seat of Christ, that each one may receive the things done in the body, according to what he has done, whether good or bad." You are going to the platform to receive your rewards for serving the Lord, for faithfulness of service. You may think, *Well, nobody knows me. Nobody really understands what I do for God.* God does. God keeps the record book, and you will not go unrewarded for all the unseen actions you have done in the name of Jesus.

This promise runs all the way through Scripture. Yes, there will be the challenge of loss of rewards and loss of opportunities perhaps. However, the truth is that we're all headed to the bema seat where the Lord Himself will give those final rewards. When I go to heaven, I'm going to see Jesus, right in the Father's house at the judgment seat of Christ. As a believer, you will too. We need to ask ourselves, "What would we like to hear our Lord say?" I want to hear Him say, "Well done, good and faithful servant" (Matthew 25:21,23). It is interesting Jesus said, "Good and faithful servant." He didn't say, "Good and successful servant." He didn't say, "Good and famous servant." He said, "Good and faithful servant."

Greg Laurie observes the importance of our faithful service:

> Jesus told the story of a wealthy man who went on a journey (see Matthew 25:14-30). As he left, he called his servants and gave to each of them a small amount of money. He told them to invest it while he was away. Two of the three servants did invest the money, and it multiplied. To those two faithful servants the master said, "Well done, good and faithful servant; you were faithful over a few

things, I will make you ruler over many things. Enter into the joy of your lord" (Matthew 25:21).

Notice that those who were faithful were rewarded accordingly. But notice one more thing: their rewards were more opportunities to serve. If you are faithful in the little things, God will give you other opportunities to do greater things.[2]

Your faithfulness will be rewarded by the Lord Himself. God is keeping the record.

4. The Marriage of the Lamb

Fourth, we are headed to a wedding! One day, we will attend the marriage of the Lamb in heaven. Revelation 19 builds to this great climax before the return of Christ when the apostle John speaks about this future marriage. The chapter opens with a chorus of hallelujahs. Then it says in Revelation 19:7, "Let us be glad and rejoice and give Him glory, for the marriage of the Lamb has come, and His wife has made herself ready." The context of this marriage is clearly pictured as taking place in heaven.

How did the church get there? There had to be a rapture. There must be a time when the church goes *up* in the rapture to go to the marriage in heaven. The rapture must precede this event. At the marriage of the Lamb, you will receive a white robe, the gift of righteousness from Christ Himself. Did you ever ask yourself, "Why do brides in the Western world wear white dresses?" The tradition is right out of the book of Revelation. It is the destiny of the true believer.

The bride of Christ is going to be adorned in a robe of white. We will receive a gift of righteousness we do not deserve, did not earn, and cannot work to obtain. We can only receive it by His grace. It is a gift to us and we receive it by faith. It's God's gift to our response of faith. He provides it. We receive it and all of heaven rejoices. No matter what your experience has been on earth—married a long time, a short time, several times, or not at all—as a believer you are headed to the greatest marriage of all time: the ceremony of the spiritual union of the believers with Jesus Christ in heaven.

5. The Return of Christ

Fifth, we have the hope of the return of Jesus Christ. At the end of the tribulation period, the world will be a mess. When humanity is at its lowest point, Christ will come to make things right. Revelation 19:11-16 describes this heavenly procession. Many people do not realize we will return *with* Him! Jesus will no longer be riding a donkey as He did on Palm Sunday. He will return on a white horse in triumph. There is a two-sided message in the book of Revelation. It contains a message of hope for the believer, but a message of judgment for the unbeliever. This great climax of Revelation 19 begins with four hallelujahs (vv. 1-6). Heaven rejoices over the fall of the kingdoms of the world and the coming of the Savior.

Then the reader is introduced to the marriage of the church to Christ in heaven. Revelation 19:7-8 says:

> "Let us be glad and rejoice and give Him glory, for the marriage of the Lamb has come, and His wife has made herself ready." And to her it was granted to be arrayed in fine linen, clean and bright, for the fine linen is the righteous acts of the saints.

The church will go up to heaven in the rapture to return with Christ *after* the marriage of the Lamb.

While angels will attend Christ at His return (Matthew 25:31), this is the church, the bride of Christ, marching out of heaven with her warrior husband in triumph in Revelation 19:11-16. It is no longer a persecuted or martyred church, but a victorious church. The raptured church has gone to the marriage. She returns in triumph, marches out of heaven with her warrior husband to reign and rule in His kingdom on earth. One writer notes, "The word [*armies*] is in the plural number, meaning that at least two separate armies will return with Him. One army is known as *hosts of the Lord*, or the angelic army [Mat. 16:27]... Another army that will return with Jesus is the army of the Church saints who had been raptured previously."[3]

Jesus will have the words written on his thigh "KING OF KINGS

AND LORD OF LORDS." He will speak the word at the battle of Armageddon and eliminate the army of the Antichrist. He will not fight with guns and tanks and bombs. He who spoke the world into existence will *speak* and the battle will be over. It will be the battle that never is a battle. He will slay the enemy with the word of His mouth (v. 15). He will then take the beast and the false prophet and cast them alive into the lake of fire, and Satan will be bound in the abyss for a thousand years (Revelation 19:19–20:3).

Won't it be great to live in a world where Satan is bound? Scripture gives us numerous examples of the ways Satan attacks believers:

- Satan filled the heart of Ananias to lie to the Holy Spirit, resulting in the death of him and his wife (Acts 5:3).

- Paul said that Satan is blinding the eyes of nonbelievers in this current age so that they should not receive the gospel (2 Corinthians 4:3-4).

- Paul told the Corinthians that Satan transforms himself (deceptively) into an angel of light (2 Corinthians 11:14).

- Paul was given a thorn in the flesh, "a messenger of Satan" to attack his body (2 Corinthians 12:7).

- Paul told the Ephesians that Satan, the prince of the power of the air, "now works in the sons of disobedience" (Ephesians 2:2).

- Paul told the Ephesians not to give place to the devil (Ephesians 4:27) and that they wrestled against "spiritual hosts of wickedness in the heavenly places" (Ephesians 6:12).

- Paul was hindered by Satan from visiting the Thessalonian church (1 Thessalonians 2:18).

- The coming of the lawless one, the Antichrist, will be "according to the working of Satan, with all power, signs and lying wonders" (2 Thessalonians 2:9). This is fulfilled, in part, by the activities of the false prophet documented in the book of Revelation.

- Paul delivered Hymenaeus and Alexander to Satan so that they might learn not to blaspheme (1 Timothy 1:20).

- James warns believers to submit to God and resist the devil (James 4:7).

- Peter warns believers to be sober and vigilant because "your adversary the devil walks about like a roaring lion, seeking whom he may devour" (1 Peter 5:8).

- John tells us that "the whole world lies under the sway of the wicked one" (1 John 5:19).

- Satan is a source of deception and rebellion throughout the events of the book of Revelation (Revelation 12:9; 13:14; 19:20; 20:7-10).[4]

This epic battle will end Satan's influence in our world, binding him for a thousand years. Only after the millennial reign of Christ will Satan be allowed one final desperate act of rebellion before his eternal judgment and condemnation in the lake of fire (Revelation 20:10).

6. The Millennial Reign

The sixth thing promised in the believer's future is the millennial reign with Christ on earth. After defeating His enemies at Armageddon, Jesus will enter Jerusalem and begin reigning from His rightful throne for a thousand years. This period of time, called the millennial reign or millennial kingdom, is described in Revelation 20:1-6:

> Then I saw an angel coming down from heaven, having the key to the bottomless pit and a great chain in his hand. He laid hold of the dragon, that serpent of old, who is the Devil and Satan, and bound him for a thousand years; and he cast him into the bottomless pit, and shut him up, and set a seal on him, so that he should deceive the nations no

more till the thousand years were finished. But after these things he must be released for a little while.

And I saw thrones, and they sat on them, and judgment was committed to them. Then I saw the souls of those who had been beheaded for their witness to Jesus and for the word of God, who had not worshiped the beast or his image, and had not received his mark on their foreheads or on their hands. And they lived and reigned with Christ for a thousand years. But the rest of the dead did not live again until the thousand years were finished. This is the first resurrection. Blessed and holy is he who has part in the first resurrection. Over such the second death has no power, but they shall be priests of God and of Christ, and shall reign with Him a thousand years.

Satan is bound and the saints reign and rule with Christ. This will include the resurrected Old Testament saints, because Jesus said He would sit down in the kingdom with Abraham, Isaac, and Jacob to drink the fruit of the vine again with the people of Israel when they say, "Blessed is he who comes in the name of the Lord!"

Those who seek to offer an alternative view supporting a nonliteral amillennialism must find a way to deal with the fact that these verses emphasize a literal thousand-year period six times. The church will be there, the Old Testament saints will be there, and the tribulation saints will be there.

As great as the millennial kingdom will be, however, it will not be the end. After this thousand-year period, Satan, who will never repent, will make one final rebellion and be thrown into the lake of fire forever, leading to the seventh and most glorious part of our amazing future.

7. The New Heavens and Earth

Our seventh future promise is the glorious eternal city, the New Jerusalem. Author Ron Rhodes has noted, "Each of us likely already has an idea regarding what heaven might be like. The chances are, though, that our culturally influenced conceptions are woefully inadequate to capture the full glory and splendor of what truly awaits the children of God in the afterlife."[5]

The final two chapters of the Bible provide our best description of the new heaven, new earth, and new heavenly city where there will be no more curse or sin. The details of our eternity future are beyond understanding, leaving the apostle John saying, "Lord Jesus, come quickly" (see Revelation 22:20). Norman Geisler emphasizes the duration of heaven, saying:

> Heaven will endure as long as God does, and God is eternal; heaven is where we will experience eternal life in its fullness. Further, heaven is the fulfillment of God's promised everlasting life to believers, "the hope of eternal life, which God, who does not lie, promised before the beginning of time" (Titus 1:2). Jesus said, "The righteous [will go] to eternal life" (Matt. 25:46), and John declared, "I heard every creature in heaven and on earth and under the earth and on the sea, and all that is in them, singing: 'To him who sits on the throne and to the Lamb be praise and honor and glory and power, for ever and ever!'" (Rev. 5:13).[6]

The book of Revelation ends by introducing us to eternity—the eternal city, the New Jerusalem, that will last forever and ever (also Hebrews 11:13-16). Paradise is regained, and the tree of life will be there. There will be no death, no sorrow, no pain, and no sin. What will be there? God and the Lamb. They will be the light and the glory of the eternal city. They will be the temple, because we will see Him face-to-face and have an audience with the King, living in His presence forever and ever.

Just Getting Started

These are the seven amazing things you can look forward to in your future if you know the Lord as your Savior. If you aren't sure where you stand with Jesus, this is where you must begin. He called on people to repent, believe, and follow Him (Luke 24:47; John 11:25;

Matthew 16:24). He simply asks you to do the same. Romans 10:9 teaches, "If you confess with your mouth the Lord Jesus and believe in your heart that God has raised Him from the dead, you will be saved."

When you do believe, 1 John 5:13 tells us we can have confidence in the Lord's power to save us: "These things I have written to you who believe in the name of the Son of God, that you may know that you have eternal life, and that you may continue to believe in the name of the Son of God." Scripture was written to help us know we have eternal life. This eternal life begins the moment we believe in Jesus and it extends to eternity future as we experience God's amazing plan for our eternal lives.

God Is with You in Tough Times

In the meantime, we may still face life's challenges. Many respond in fear, yet as believers, we can trust that God is with us in tough times. The Father's promises are for both time and eternity. In his second letter to the Christians in Corinth, Paul gave words of comfort. He reminded them as he reminds us of several important truths.

Reality (2 Corinthians 1:3-5)

Trouble is a part of life in a fallen world. We all deal with it time and again. Everybody has problems. Abraham lied. Moses fled. Elijah hid. Peter denied. Paul suffered. But despite his suffering, Paul reminds us God is the Father of mercies and the God of all comfort (v. 3). He comforts us in all our troubles (v. 4), not from them. Suffering is part of God's purifying work in our lives. Peter tells us that believers are often called to suffer for the cause of Christ and the sake of the gospel (1 Peter 1:17-21).

Resolve (2 Corinthians 1:6-7)

Problems change us one way or the other. Pain can make us bitter or better. Peter's failure led to his tears of repentance and his ultimate restoration (Luke 22:61-62; John 21:15-17). Judas's betrayal led only to remorse and suicide (Matthew 27:3-5). In each case, we learn there is a right way and a wrong way to deal with our problems and failures. Whatever we decide to do in the face of crisis will make us better or bitter. The choice is up to us. We must resolve to face each challenge with God's help. Paul could say whether we are *afflicted* or *comforted* we will receive the *consolation and salvation* of God Himself (vv. 6-7).

Resource (2 Corinthians 1:8-10)

Our problems and suffering cause us to turn to God for help. Challenges like a global pandemic make us realize we cannot trust in ourselves alone for the answer. When we are in trouble, pressed beyond measure, despair even of life, or like Paul, feel we have the sentence of death (vv. 8-9), we can only trust in God who has delivered us (in the past) and delivers us (in the present) and will yet deliver us in the future (v. 10). He alone is our ultimate resource in times of trouble.

Relationships (2 Corinthians 1:11-12)

While God is our ultimate resource, He works through our relationships with other believers to encourage us. As Paul faced his own problems, he reminded the believers they had helped him in two significant ways to endure his suffering. First, he said, "You also helping together in prayer for us." In times of trouble we need to know that other believers are praying for us. I need your prayers and you need to know I am praying for you. Second, Paul said that their gift helped him to carry on God's work on their behalf (v. 11).

What can we learn from 2 Corinthians 1:3-11?

1. Everybody has problems.
2. God is greater than our problems.
3. God can overrule our problems.
4. God can use our problems to His glory.
5. He will comfort us in all our troubles.
6. We must choose how we will respond when trouble comes.
7. God will ultimately deliver us from our problems.

Several years ago, my granddaughter Jennifer Barrick was severely injured in a terrible accident. Her family was hit by a drunk driver fleeing the police in a high-speed chase. Jennifer suffered multiple traumatic brain injuries and hovered between life and death for several months.

As she lay in a coma, unconscious of the world around her, Jen carried on an intimate conversation with the Lord. She talked to Jesus constantly as if He were right there with her. Her mind and body were injured but the Holy Spirit in her was not. He continued to soothe and comfort her over the weeks that followed.

Months later when Jen miraculously began to recover, she continued that same intimate conservation with God. And now, years later it still flows from her heart and soul. Today, as I finished writing this chapter, she texted me this prayer. And I felt led to share it with you.

> Abundant Father, my heart finds rest in You and Your Truth. Thank you for being a True and Faithful KING. I run to you for strength, courage and direction. My prayer is that You would LEAD, GUIDE and DIRECT me every step of the way! Over my day today I want to pray Philippians 4:13, "I can do ALL THINGS through CHRIST who strengthens me." WOW! That is so reassuring. Take charge of my day GOOD SHEPHERD! TRUSTING You as we go together to:
>
> The Promised Land
>
> The Eternal City
>
> The Father's House

2

THE RAPTURE:
AT ANY MOMENT?

Most Christians believe Jesus is coming again. In fact, virtually all Christian denominations affirm the second coming of Christ. They simply differ on *when* and *how* He will come. As a result, they also differ on *what* we should be doing in the meantime. Since our beliefs motivate our behaviors they really do matter. Those of us who believe Jesus could come at any moment are motivated to make a difference in our world sooner rather than later.

In our book *Can We Still Believe in the Rapture?* Mark Hitchcock and I note the Scriptures describe the coming of Jesus as imminent. Imminence is generally defined as an "any moment" view of the rapture. Gerald Stanton notes, "As applied to the coming of the Lord, imminency consists of three things: the certainty that he may come at any moment, the uncertainty of the time of that arrival, and the fact that no prophesied event stands between the believer and that hour."[1]

New Testament scholar Robert Gundry further explains, "By common consent imminence means that so far as we know no predicted event will necessarily precede the coming of Christ."[2] John Sproule adds, "Christ can return for His Church at any moment and that no predicted event will intervene before that return."[3] To which I would add that no predicted event *must* intervene. It is possible that certain predicted events *might* occur before the rapture, but no specific event *must* precede the rapture.

One day, without warning, the Spirit of God will move, the trumpet will sound, the archangel will shout, and the Bible tells us Christ will come and rapture believers home to heaven. We as believers look forward to this event that will mark the beginning of the amazing future God has in store for us. The Bible clearly teaches:

> But I do not want you to be ignorant, brethren, concerning those who have fallen asleep, lest you sorrow as others who have no hope. For if we believe that Jesus died and rose again, even so God will bring with Him those who sleep in Jesus (1 Thessalonians 4:13-14).

When a believer dies, his or her body goes to the grave. But the person's spirit goes to heaven. The apostle Paul described the believer's experience at death as "to be absent from the body and to be present with the Lord" (2 Corinthians 5:8). At the time of the rapture, our spirit will return with Christ. Our body will be resurrected, reunited with our spirit, and then we will literally be taken, body and spirit, home to the Father's house. Paul continues, stating:

> For the Lord Himself will descend from heaven with a shout, with the voice of an archangel, and with the trumpet of God. And the dead in Christ will rise first. Then we who are alive and remain shall be caught up together with them in the clouds to meet the Lord in the air. And thus we shall always be with the Lord. Therefore comfort one another with these words (1 Thessalonians 4:16-18).

Here is a message of comfort and encouragement for the believer. Jesus said to the disciples on the last night before He suffered on the cross, "I go to prepare a place for you. And if I go and prepare a place for you, I will come again and receive you to Myself; that where I am, there you may be also" (John 14:2-3). That is the promise of the rapture, to "be caught up" as it says in the King James Version. Suddenly we will be snatched away, caught up to be with our Savior.

There are some things we do not know concerning the details, but the big picture of Bible prophecy is clear. One day the Lord is coming for those of us who believe. When the rapture occurs, it will change everything.

What Is the Rapture?

We've talked about the rapture, but what is it exactly? The Bible clearly teaches there is a future time when Christ will return for His people. Notice, for example, 1 Thessalonians 4:15-18, where the apostle Paul provides us with these details:

> This we say to you by the word of the Lord, that we who are alive and remain until the coming of the Lord will by no means precede those who are asleep. For the Lord Himself will descend from heaven with a shout, with the voice of an archangel, and with the trumpet of God. And the dead in Christ will rise first. Then we who are alive and remain shall be caught up together with them in the clouds to meet the Lord in the air. And thus we shall always be with the Lord. Therefore comfort one another with these words.

From this passage of Scripture, we can see that there are five stages to the rapture:

1. The Lord Himself will descend from heaven with a shout and with the sound of a trumpet.

2. The dead in Christ will rise first.

3. Then we who are alive and remain on earth will be caught up together with them in the clouds.

4. We all will meet the Lord in the air.

5. And we will always be with Him.

The English word *rapture* comes from the Latin *rapto*, which is a translation of the word *harpazo* in the Greek New Testament. All these terms mean "caught up" or "snatched away." They describe God's action in "physically and miraculously transporting people from one place to another."[4] While the word *rapture* does not appear in English translations, the concept of the rapture certainly does. Biblical examples include Enoch (Genesis 5:24), Elijah (2 Kings 2:11), and the two witnesses (Revelation 11:3-12).[5] It is a sudden and instantaneous event that will occur without warning.

The apostle Paul also unveiled what he referred to as a "mystery" pertaining to the rapture. He explained that there will be some Christians who will not sleep (die), but whose bodies will be instantly transformed:

> Behold, I tell you a mystery: We shall not all sleep, but we shall all be changed—in a moment, in the twinkling of an eye, at the last trumpet. For the trumpet will sound, and the dead will be raised incorruptible, and we shall be changed. For this corruptible must put on incorruption, and this mortal must put on immortality (1 Corinthians 15:51-53).

At the moment of the rapture, the bodies of all believers who have died with faith in Christ since the Day of Pentecost will suddenly be transformed into new, living, immortal, resurrected bodies. Even those whose bodies have long since decayed or whose ashes have been scattered across the oceans will receive a new body. This new body will be joined together with the person's spirit, which Jesus brings with Him from heaven. Then the bodies of those who are alive on earth and have accepted Christ as their Savior will also be instantly translated into new, glorified immortal bodies.

Notice the similarity of the descriptions of the rapture in 1 Corinthians 15:51-53 and 1 Thessalonians 4:15-18. When Christ comes to take His church (all believers) to heaven in fulfillment of His promise in John 14:1-3, He will include all New Testament believers, both the living and the dead. Paul seems to have this in mind in 2 Corinthians 4:14 as well when he writes: "Knowing that he who raised the Lord Jesus will raise us also with Jesus and bring us with you into his presence" (ESV).

Together, all believers will be instantaneously transported into heaven to meet their saved loved ones "in the clouds" and then to meet the Lord in the air. Those who have rejected the salvation of Jesus Christ and remain on earth will witness a miraculous event of astonishing proportions—the sudden mass disappearance of millions upon millions of Christians from the face of the earth. While critics of the rapture teaching often object to it as a "secret rapture," there won't be anything secret about it! The unbelieving world will be in a state of shock, far worse than during the recent pandemic.

The rapture is often referred to as "the blessed hope" (Titus 2:13) because it provides comfort not only to those believers who are concerned about the coming tribulation, but also to those who long to be reunited with their departed loved ones who share faith in Christ.

The second coming, which encompasses both the rapture and the glorious appearing, is one of the most significant events mentioned in the entire Bible. There are 321 references in the New Testament alone to this awesome event, making it the second most prominent doctrine presented in Scripture after the doctrine of salvation.

The concept of the second coming is clearly taught in both the Old and New Testaments. On average, the New Testament mentions the second coming in one out of every thirty verses, and it is mentioned in every chapter of 1 and 2 Thessalonians, most likely the first books written for the early church. In addition, all nine New Testament authors mention the second coming, and twenty-three of the twenty-seven New Testament books reference it. God clearly intended His church to be motivated to holiness and world evangelism by the study of the second coming of Jesus Christ. Since Jesus is coming again, we are called to live for Christ with urgency and to talk about Him with everyone we can.

The Phases of the Second Coming

Much confusion exists among Bible readers regarding the second coming of Christ. Of central importance is whether Jesus will return once or twice. There are clearly two phases to the second coming, no matter what one's view is of the timing between them. Jesus is coming *for* believers in the air (rapture) and *with* believers (return) to the earth. I believe it is better to speak of the return of Christ as one of the phases of the second coming. When the biblical references pertaining to the second coming are carefully examined, it becomes clear that there are not two second comings but two distinct phases to Christ's return: 1) the rapture of the church, and 2) the return of Christ with the church.

Remember, there were also multiple events related to the first coming of Christ: His birth, life, ministry, death, burial, resurrection, and ascension. These were all part of the first coming of Christ. Further, there are simply too many conflicting elements in these phases of the second coming to merge them into a single event. In the first phase, Jesus will come suddenly to rapture His church in the air and take all believers to His Father's house in fulfillment of His promise in John 14:1-3. There, they will appear before the judgment seat of Christ (2 Corinthians 5:9-10) and participate in the marriage supper of the Lamb (Revelation 19:1-10).

During this time, those left behind on the earth will experience the trials of the horrendous seven-year interval referred to as the tribulation. Paul distinguishes between these two phases in Titus 2:13, where he refers to the rapture as "the blessed hope" and the return of Christ to the earth as the "glorious appearing."

Some theologians attempt to dismiss these multiple phases of Christ's second coming. They place both the rapture and the glorious appearing at the end of the tribulation and hold to what is known as the posttribulation view of the rapture. In this scenario, Christians will be required to face the horrors of the tribulation. However, this view teaches that Christ (the bridegroom) will virtually beat up the church (His bride) in order to prepare her for their heavenly marriage!

To hold this view, one must ignore numerous passages of Scripture. A careful study of the many biblical references to the second coming clearly shows that the rapture and the glorious appearing are two separate phases of the second coming. Consider the following differences:

The Rapture of the Church	The Glorious Appearing
1. Christ comes for believers in the air.	1. Christ comes with believers to the earth.
2. All Christians on earth are translated into new bodies.	2. There is no translation of bodies.
3. Christians are taken to the Father's house in heaven.	3. Resurrected saints remain on the earth.
4. There is no judgment upon the earth.	4. Christ judges the inhabitants of the earth.
5. The church will be taken to heaven.	5. Christ sets up His kingdom on earth.
6. It could occur at any time (it is imminent).	6. It cannot occur until the end of the seven-year tribulation period.
7. There are no signs preceding it.	7. There are numerous signs preceding it.
8. It affects only believers.	8. It affects all humanity.
9. It is a time of joy.	9. It is a time of mourning.
10. It occurs before the "day of wrath."	10. It occurs after the "day of wrath."
11. Satan is not bound but wreaks havoc on the earth.	11. Satan is bound in the abyss for a thousand years.
12. Christians are judged at the judgment seat of Christ.	12. Christians have already been judged at the judgment seat.
13. The marriage of the Lamb takes place.	13. The marriage of the Lamb has already taken place.
14. Only Christ's own will see Him.	14. All those on earth will see Him.
15. The seven-year tribulation follows.	15. The thousand-year millennium follows.

When Will the Rapture Occur?

While various views exist as to *when* the rapture will occur (before, during, or after the tribulation), all must acknowledge that there will be a rapture. The only real question is, "When will it occur?" Christ must return at some point to resurrect the "dead in Christ" and rapture living believers to take us all to the Father's house in heaven, as Jesus promised in John 14:1-4. There are several reasons to believe the rapture will occur *before* the tribulation begins:

1. The Lord Himself promised to deliver us. Revelation 3:10 says, "Because you have kept My command to persevere, I also will keep you from the hour of trial which shall come upon the whole world, to test those who dwell on the earth." The Greek work *ek*, which literally means "out of," is translated in this passage as "from." In other words, it is the Lord's intention to keep the church *out of* the tribulation. Therefore, the rapture must occur before the tribulation begins.

2. The church is to be delivered from the wrath to come. Paul tells us in 1 Thessalonians 1:10 that we should "wait for His Son from heaven, whom He raised from the dead, even Jesus who delivers us from the wrath to come." The context of this passage is also the rapture. The church must therefore be removed from the earth before the tribulation begins in order to be delivered from the wrath to come.

3. The church is not appointed to wrath. According to 1 Thessalonians 5:9, "God did not appoint us to wrath, but to obtain salvation through our Lord Jesus Christ." Once again, the context of this passage is the rapture. Since the tribulation is prophesied as a time of God's wrath, and since Christians are not appointed to wrath, it follows that the church must be raptured out of the way before the tribulation begins. Verse 4 indicates that "Day" will come suddenly and unexpectedly like a "thief."

4. The church is absent in Revelation chapters 4–18. These chapters detail the events of the tribulation. The church is mentioned seventeen times in the first three chapters of Revelation, but after John (who is a member of the church) is taken up to heaven at the beginning of chapter 4, the church is not mentioned or seen again until chapter 19.

Then it appears at the marriage with Christ in heaven and subsequently returns to earth with Jesus at His glorious appearing. Why is the church missing from those chapters? The most likely scenario is because the church doesn't go through the tribulation, having been raptured away before the tribulation begins.

5. If the church is raptured at the end of the tribulation, there will be no believers left to repopulate the earth during the millennium. Just before the millennial kingdom begins, all sinners (those who reject Jesus Christ as Savior) who have survived the tribulation will be cast into hell, according to Matthew 25:46. If the rapture occurs at the end of the tribulation, as some believe, all Christians would be taken from the earth as well, leaving no one on earth with a natural body to repopulate the planet during the millennium.

The problem here is that numerous Old Testament passages, as well as Revelation 20:7-10, note there will be a huge population explosion during the millennium. Where will these people come from? The best answer is that many of those who miss the rapture and become believers during the tribulation (thanks to the preaching of the 144,000 Jews and the two witnesses) will survive to the end of the tribulation and will repopulate the earth. While large numbers of believers will be martyred during the tribulation, many will survive. These people will not be raptured at the end of the tribulation in some sort of posttribulational rapture but will instead enter Christ's millennial kingdom with their natural bodies to populate His kingdom. For this to be possible, the rapture must take place prior to the tribulation instead of at the end of it.

6. Only the pretribulational view fulfills Jesus' simple command to "watch" until He comes (Matthew 24:42). He never told us to watch for the Antichrist, the tribulation, or the final judgment. He clearly told His disciples to watch for Him to return and to be ready for Him to come for them (v. 44). We are to live in anticipation of the fact that Jesus could come at any time.

7. The rapture before the tribulation also fulfills Jesus' statement to the disciples in the upper room when He promised to take them home to the Father's house in heaven (John 14:2-3). "I go to prepare a place for you. And if I go and prepare a place for you, I will come again and receive you to Myself; that where I am, *there* you may be also," Jesus explained. Judas had already left the room to betray Jesus. Therefore, he was not a recipient of the rapture promise that Jesus affirmed to the eleven believing disciples (cf. John 13:21-30).

Paul Benware notes that several events listed in Scripture seem to take place *after* the rapture but *before* the return of Christ to earth: 1. judgment seat of Christ, 2. marriage of the Lamb, 3. salvation of those who will populate the millennial kingdom. Benware observes: "The pretribulation rapture of the church provides the necessary time for these events to take place…but they pose serious difficulties for the posttribulation view."[6]

Among the chief features of the rapture is that it will be sudden and catch people by surprise. "Of that day and hour no one knows" (Matthew 24:36), which is why we should live as to "be ready, for the Son of Man is coming at an hour you do not expect" (v. 44). Only a pretribulation rapture preserves that any-moment expectation of His coming. Indeed, the rapture has appeared imminent to Christians of every generation. Nothing could better motivate us to holy living and fervent evangelism than to believe that Jesus could come today. One day He will! The trumpet will sound, the archangel will shout, and we will all go home to be with Jesus.

The Rapture Is a Biblical Concept

For God to rapture people to heaven is not entirely new in biblical history. It has already occurred in biblical times.

Enoch: "Enoch walked with God; and he was not, for God took him" (Genesis 5:24). The New Testament adds, "By faith Enoch was taken away so that he did not see death, 'and was not found, because God had taken him'; for before he was taken he had this testimony, that he pleased God" (Hebrews 11:5).

Elijah: "Then it happened, as they continued on and talked, that suddenly a chariot of fire appeared with horses of fire, and separated the two of them; and Elijah went up by a whirlwind into heaven" (2 Kings 2:11).

Jesus Christ: After His resurrection, Jesus ascended into heaven. "Now when He had spoken these things, while they watched, He was taken up, and a cloud received Him out of their sight. And while they looked steadfastly toward heaven as He went up, behold, two men stood by them in white apparel, who also said, 'Men of Galilee, why do you stand gazing up into heaven? This same Jesus, who was taken up from you into heaven, will so come in like manner as you saw Him go into heaven'" (Acts 1:9-11). This same event is described in Revelation 12:5, where Jesus (symbolically as the Child) is "caught up" (*harpazo*) into heaven.

Philip: "When they came up out of the water, the Spirit of the Lord snatched Philip away; and the eunuch no longer saw him, but went on his way rejoicing. But Philip found himself at Azotus, and as he passed through he kept preaching the gospel to all the cities until he came to Caesarea" (Acts 8:39-40 NASB).

Two significant observations are seen in Philip's rapture. First, it took place by the Spirit of the Lord, the Holy Spirit. This is the first mention of the third person of the Trinity involved in a rapture account. Certainly, the triune God—Father, Son, and Spirit—will be involved in the future rapture of all believers. Second, the passage notes "and the eunuch no longer saw him." Though Philip was only temporarily raptured to another location, this event highlights one important aspect of the future rapture of the church. Those remaining on the earth will no longer see them.

Paul: Second Corinthians 12:2-4 (NASB) says, "I know a man in Christ who fourteen years ago—whether in the body I do not know, or out of the body I do not know, God knows—such a man was caught up to the third heaven. And I know how such a man—whether in the body or apart from the body I do not know, God knows—was caught up into Paradise and heard inexpressible words, which a man is not permitted to speak." Most scholars believe Paul was speaking of himself, with Paul "caught up" either literally or in a rapturous vision to heaven.

John: In Revelation 4:1-2, we find, "After these things I looked, and behold, a door standing open in heaven, and the first voice which I had heard, like the sound of a trumpet speaking with me, said, 'Come

up here, and I will show you what must take place after these things.'
Immediately I was in the Spirit; and behold, a throne was standing in
heaven, and One sitting on the throne."

Most of these events describe a natural body of flesh being changed
and translated into the presence of God. In our finite bodies, we cannot enter His presence; a sudden translation of flesh to spirit becomes
necessary. In the case of both Paul and John the biblical text can certainly indicate either literal rapture or visionary experience (Revelation
1:1-2,10-11; 4:1-2).

The Power of the Rapture

Those in Christ who will be snatched up in the rapture do not have
to generate their own power to accomplish this. As in all our dealings
with God, He provides the impetus. He has not assigned our resurrection to an angel or specifically created being, for "the Lord Himself
will descend from heaven with a shout" (1 Thessalonians 4:16). In other
words, He will do the raising. In John 5:21,25-29, Jesus clearly claimed
to possess resurrection power for Himself, using it as proof that He was
God in human flesh.

Since so much is at stake here, including our eternal destiny, notice
a most comforting truth. Christ has already demonstrated His power
to raise the dead. He did it three times during His brief earthly ministry, the most dramatic of which was Lazarus in John 11:43 when He
commanded, "Lazarus, come forth!" To the astonishment of the people of Bethany, a man dead four days was delivered from his tomb.
When that same experienced voice shouts from heaven at the rapture,
all those who are in Christ by faith will respond.

The Lord Jesus Himself declared, "I am the resurrection and the life.
He who believes in Me, though he may die, he shall live. And whoever
lives and believes in Me shall never die" (John 11:25-26). For almost
two thousand years, all Christians who died immediately went in spirit
to heaven to be with Christ. As Paul said, "To be absent from the body
and to be present with the Lord" (2 Corinthians 5:8). When Christ
comes for His church, He will resurrect the bodies of deceased saints,

unite them with their soul and spirit in heaven, and translate all living believers to be with them and Him forever. No wonder the early Christians used to greet each other with "Maranatha!" (The Lord is coming!)

Many who do not believe in the pretribulational rapture falsely assume there will be *no rapture at all.* This is a complete misconception. If one takes seriously passages like 1 Thessalonians 4:17, "We who are alive and remain will be caught up together with them in the clouds to meet the Lord in the air" (NASB), he or she is forced to conclude that there will be a rapture. The only real debate is over *when* it will occur.

Arguments raised against the rapture on the basis that it is difficult to conceive of what it would be like for millions of people to suddenly disappear are irrelevant. Joking remarks about bumping your head on the ceiling, or false teeth being left behind, or hundreds of car accidents suddenly occurring are inconsequential because Scripture clearly states that we will be "caught up" into the air at some point in time.

There will be a rapture! The only serious questions are: 1) When will it occur? And 2) What is its relationship to the return of Christ at the time of His second coming?

The Time of His Coming

Most evangelicals agree as to the nature of Christ's coming, but there is substantial disagreement about the *time.* Millard Erickson observes: "The one eschatological doctrine on which orthodox theologians most agree is the second coming of Christ. It is indispensable to eschatology. It is the basis of the Christian's hope, the one event which will mark the beginning of the completion of God's plan."[7]

The New Testament picture of our Lord's return emphasizes at least six distinct aspects of the time of His coming. These may be summarized as follows:

Future

The entire emphasis of the New Testament points to a future return of Christ. He promised "I will come again" (John 14:3). The angels promised He would return (Acts 1:11). The apostles taught the certainty of His future return (Philippians 3:20-21; Titus 2:13; 2 Peter 3:3-13; 1 John 3:2-3). Clearly, He has not returned yet: The rapture has not occurred, the tribulation has not begun, and the Antichrist has not yet been revealed.

Imminent

The return of Jesus Christ is always described as potentially imminent or "at hand" (Revelation 1:3; 22:10). Every generation of believers is warned to be ready for His coming, as Luke 12:40 states: "Therefore you also be ready, for the Son of Man is coming at an hour you do not expect." Believers are constantly urged to look for the coming of the Lord (Philippians 3:20; Titus 2:13; 1 Thessalonians 5:6; Hebrews 9:28). An imminent perspective of the rapture also seems to be in mind in James 5:8-9 (NIV): "You too, be patient and stand firm, because the Lord's coming is near. Don't grumble against one another, brothers and sisters, or you will be judged. The Judge is standing at the door!" Rhodes notes:

> The term *imminent* literally means "ready to take place" or "impending." The New Testament teaches that the rapture is imminent—that is, nothing must be prophetically fulfilled before the rapture can occur…The rapture is a signless event that can occur at any moment. This is in contrast to the second coming of Christ, which is preceded by many events that transpire during the seven-year tribulation period.[8]

Distant

From God's perspective, Jesus is coming at any moment. But from the human perspective it has already been nearly two thousand years. Jesus hinted at this in the Olivet Discourse in the illustration of the man who traveled into a "far country" (heaven) and was gone "a long time" (Matthew 25:14,19). Peter also implies this in his prediction that men will begin to scoff at the idea of the second coming, after a long period of time (2 Peter 3:3-9).

Undated

While the rapture is the next major event on the prophetic calendar, it is undated, as is the glorious appearing of Christ. Jesus said: "But of that day and hour no one knows, not even the angels of heaven" (Matthew 24:36). Later He added: "It is not for you to know times or seasons which the Father has put in His own authority" (Acts 1:7). Only after the rapture will the time of Christ's appearing become clear.

Unexpected

The mass of humanity will not be looking for Christ when He returns (Matthew 24:50; Luke 21:35). So unexpected will His return be that "it will come as a snare on all those who dwell on the face of the whole earth" (Luke 21:35).

Sudden

The Bible warns that Jesus will come "as a thief in the night. For when they say, 'Peace and safety!' then sudden destruction" will come upon the unbelieving world (1 Thessalonians 5:2-3). His return for the bride will occur in a flash: "In a moment, in the twinkling of an eye, at the last trumpet. For the trumpet will sound, and the dead [believers] will be raised incorruptible, and we [living believers] shall be changed" (1 Corinthians 15:52).

The return of Christ is a series of events fulfilling all end-time prophecies of His coming. These include predictions of His coming *for* His church and His coming *with* His church. There can be no adequate system of biblical prophecy without a rapture. The church will be "caught up" and "gathered together" to the Lord (2 Thessalonians 2:1-2). The only real debate is over the question of when. And when the rapture does take place, millions of Christians will disappear in an instant, shaking those left behind and leaving a power vacuum of global proportions that will set the stage for the tribulation.

The Promise of the Bridegroom

Not only do we have the wonderful prediction of the marriage, but we also have the promise of the bridegroom Himself. In John 14, Jesus is about to go to the cross. On the night of the Last Supper, He meets with the disciples and says:

> "Let not your heart be troubled; you believe in God, believe also in Me. In My Father's house are many mansions: if it were not so, I would have told you. I go to prepare a place for you. And if I go and prepare a place for you, I will come again, and receive you to Myself; that where I am, there you may be also" (John 14:1-3).

Jesus is using the language of the Jewish wedding to illustrate His relationship to the disciples. He is saying to them, "I am getting ready to go to the Father's house—heaven—where there are many mansions or palatial rooms." This is just like a Jewish bridegroom who would make a commitment to the bride to marry her. He would leave, go back to his father's house, and add some rooms to the house or build a house for the bride so he had a place to take her at the time of the marriage. Then he would come back for her, consummate the marriage, and take her home to the father's house. That is exactly what Jesus is talking about in this passage of Scripture, so that you and I have the anticipation of the fact that when Jesus comes again, He is coming uniquely for His bride. He reminds us, "I will come for you."

The promise of the rapture of the church is clearly emphasized in this passage of Scripture. Jesus is not only coming back one day to judge the world. Prior to that, He is coming in the rapture to take the bride home to the Father's house. A Savior who loves you that much is worthy of your heart, your soul, your life, and your commitment to Him. He wants to do something special for you. He wants to do something unique in your life that leads up to that marriage, to prepare you for the marriage.

The Rapture and the Book of Revelation

One concern among interpreters of Bible prophecy is the timing of the rapture within the book of Revelation. While the rapture will clearly take place at some point after the messages to the seven churches in chapters 2 and 3, debate surrounds the placement of this event in the sequence of the prophetic timeline. At least three compelling reasons exist to place the rapture with the beginning of Revelation 4.

The Location: Heaven

Revelation 4:1 begins, "After these things I looked, and behold, a door standing open in heaven." John enters, following a voice "like a trumpet" to see what will happen at some point after the messages to the seven churches. Revelation 4:2 again mentions the scene in heaven: "Immediately I was in the Spirit; and behold, a throne set in heaven, and One sat on the throne."

In addition to the One on the throne (God the Father) and the angelic creatures, John saw twenty-four elders robed in white and wearing crowns of gold (4:4). Their presence in heaven pictures raptured believers who have already received their rewards in heaven. In the next chapter, they are pictured as those who have been redeemed from every tribe, tongue, people, and nation and who will reign with Christ on the earth (5:9-10).

In chapter 5, heaven is mentioned two more times. Verse 3 speaks of the scroll in heaven, stating, "And no one in heaven or on the earth or under the earth was able to open the scroll, or to look at it." Verse 13 adds, "And every creature which is in heaven and on the earth and under the earth and such as are in the sea, and all that are in them" joined in worship to the Lamb.

The shift in focus from earth in chapters 2 and 3 to heaven in chapters 4 and 5 is also highlighted in the promise of Revelation 3:10: "Because you have kept My command to persevere, I also will keep you from the hour of trial which shall come upon the whole world, to test those who dwell on the earth." Believers are told they will escape "the hour of trial," an indication that seems to refer to the tribulation period.

The Timing: The Tribulation

Another important reason to place the rapture at Revelation 4 is the timing of the rapture. In Revelation 1–3, the church is referred to sixteen times, with the word translated "church" (*ekklesia*) used seven times. However, the church is not mentioned at all in chapters 6–18. Revelation 4 and 5 take place in heaven, where some of the aspects may refer to the church (twenty-four elders and the great multitude). Chapters 6–18 cover the seven-year tribulation period, where any mention of the church is absent. Only in Revelation 19 do church believers appear again at the marriage (vv. 7-9) and return from the Father's house (heaven) as the bride of Christ, alongside her husband at Armageddon (v. 14). In both cases the bride is described wearing white. Thomas Ice states:

> Revelation 3:10 notes that the Tribulation will not be for the church but for "those who dwell upon the earth" (Rev. 3:10; 6:10; 8:13; 11:10 [twice]; 13:8, 12, 14 [twice]; 17:2, 8), as a time upon them for their rejection of Christ [and] His salvation. While the church will experience tribulation in general during this present age (John 16:33), she is never mentioned as participating in Israel's time of trouble, which includes the Great Tribulation, the Day of the Lord, and the Wrath of God. Pretribulationism gives the best answer to the biblical explanation of the fact that the church is never mentioned in passages that speak about tribulational events, while Israel is mentioned consistently throughout these passages.[9]

Yet even more can be noted regarding the importance of Revelation 3:10. The context refers to Jesus coming quickly (3:11), giving crowns, and deliverance from judgment. Stanton observes:

> In the words "I come quickly" [3:11] may be seen the rapture, and the reference to "thy crown" [3:11] suggests the Bema seat judgment to follow. "Because thou hast kept the word of my patience, I also will keep thee from the hour of temptation, which shall come upon all the world, to try them that dwell upon the earth." Here, then, is a

promise which clearly indicates the pretribulation rapture of the Church.[10]

Finally, many scholars who hold that Revelation 3:10 refers to the rapture do so based on the use of the Greek preposition *ek* that is translated "from." Believers will not endure or experience the trials of the tribulation in any way, dismissing the views of the midtribulation, posttribulation, partial, or prewrath rapture views. Only within the pretribulation view can this interpretation be held. Dwight Pentecost argues:

> Since *ek* is used here it would indicate that John is promising a removal from the sphere of testing, not a preservation through it. This is further substantiated by the use of the words "the hour." God is not only guarding from the trials but from the very hour itself when these trials will come on those earth dwellers.[11]

The Focus: Israel

We've already mentioned the emphasis in Revelation on Old Testament prophecy. In chapters 4–18, the focus on Jewish prophecies highlights an emphasis on Israel during the tribulation period. Just as the time from the Day of Pentecost to the rapture covers the church age with an emphasis on Gentiles, the tribulation period will highlight the response of the Jewish people to the Messiah.

For example, following the six seal judgments in Revelation 6, the seventh chapter focuses on the "sealed" of Israel. This will include 144,000 Jewish male evangelists, 12,000 from each tribe, who will lead in sharing the message of the Messiah to God's people. In Revelation 11, two Jewish witnesses also will appear in Jerusalem. They will prophesy for the first half of the seven-year tribulation period to proclaim God's truth to the world, especially to the Jewish people. At the midpoint of the tribulation, the rebuilt Jewish temple in Jerusalem will be desecrated by the Antichrist (Matthew 24:15), followed by great persecution of the Jewish people in Revelation 12 and following.

LaHaye also suggests a fourth reason, noting the similarities between

Revelation 4:1-2 and other rapture passages. Believing that John's being called up to heaven pictures the rapture, he notes, "The Rapture of the Church is not explicitly taught in Revelation 4 but definitely appears here chronologically at the end of the Church Age and before the Tribulation."[12]

Based on the evidence, Renald Showers concludes in his book *Maranatha: Our Lord Come!:*

> The languages in Jesus' reference to this future period of worldwide testing implied that it was well-known to the church saints. It was well-known because both Old and New Testament Scriptures, written years before Revelation, foretold this unique, future period of testing or Tribulation, which would take place prior to the coming of the Messiah to rule the world in the Messianic Age or Millennium.[13]

Delivered from the Wrath to Come

The New Testament also offers evidence of believers escaping the tribulation based on its statements regarding our escape from wrath. Since believers in the church age will escape "the wrath of the Lamb" and "the great day of His wrath" (Revelation 6:15-17), the rapture must take place before this time. For example, Paul notes:

> Romans 5:9: "Much more then, having now been justified by His blood, we shall be saved from wrath through Him."

> 1 Thessalonians 1:9b-10: "How you turned to God from idols to serve the living and true God, and to wait for His Son from heaven, whom He raised from the dead, even Jesus who delivers us from the wrath to come."

> 1 Thessalonians 5:9: "For God did not appoint us to wrath, but to obtain salvation through our Lord Jesus Christ."

In contrast, there will be "earth dwellers" during the tribulation period.

This phrase is first mentioned in Revelation 3:10 and is used a total of eleven times in Revelation. Ice writes:

> When we survey the eleven uses of "earth dwellers" in Revelation, we see an interesting composite that develops. Not only are they to be tested in order show their true metal (3:10), they are clearly identified as those who are persecuting and killing believers during the tribulation (6:10). Many of the judgments of the tribulation are targeted for the "earth dwellers" (8:13). It is the "earth dwellers" who rejoice and send gifts to one another when the two witnesses are killed in Jerusalem during the middle of the tribulation (11:10). When the Beast (Antichrist) is introduced in Revelation 13, it is noted that, "all who dwell on the earth will worship him" (13:8, 12). Thus, 100% of the "earth dwellers" receive the mark of the beast and will spend eternity in the Lake of Fire. During the tribulation, as followers of the Beast, the "earth dwellers" will be deceived by the false signs and wonders of the Beast and will erect an image of the Beast, likely in the Jewish Temple (13:14). While the target of the preaching of the gospel by an angelic messenger will be "earth dwellers" (14:6), not a single one of the will follow the Lamb, instead they will wonder after the Beast (17:8).[14]

The contrast is clear between believers who escape the wrath to come at the rapture and those who will remain on the earth and experience the judgments of God's wrath in the tribulation. This is the great distinction between the destiny of believers and that of unbelievers: While unbelievers will suffer the wrath of God's tribulation judgments, believers can face the future with confidence in the grace of God and the hope of the rapture.

How Should We Live in the Meantime?

The timing of the rapture is in God's hands. From a human standpoint, it may appear that we are on the threshold of the final frontier.

We as believers can face the future with great confidence because we know the One who holds the future. The tension of living for today and looking forward to tomorrow is one of the realities of the Christian life. Believers find themselves caught between living here and now and joyously anticipating the glorious future God has planned for us for all eternity.

The Bible not only tells us how to prepare for the future, it also tells us how to live right now to the glory of God. As long as we remain on earth, we have a job to do and a destiny to fulfill.

At the height of World War II, Dietrich Bonhoeffer was imprisoned for taking a stand against Adolf Hitler. Yet he continued to urge fellow believers to resist Nazi tyranny. A group of Christians, believing that Hitler was the Antichrist, asked Bonhoeffer, "Why do you expose yourself to all this danger? Jesus will return any day, and all your work and suffering will be for nothing." Bonhoeffer replied, "If Jesus returns tomorrow, then tomorrow I'll rest from my labor. But today I have work to do. I must continue the struggle until it's finished."[15]

Whether our Lord returns today or years into the future, we can face each day of our lives secure in His incredible promises. If we live, we live to the glory of God. If we die, we die to the glory of God. Either way, one day we will hear the angelic shout and the trumpet call of God and *Voosh!* We are on our way to all the rest that God has planned for our amazing future.

3

THE FATHER'S HOUSE: WHAT HAPPENS WHEN WE ARRIVE?

There is something about human nature that often leaves us longing for more. We can never seem to get enough of life. We want more time. More experiences. More friends. More pleasures. More opportunities. Some of us actually wish we could start all over again.

"I just don't like the way I look," a lady once told me. "I don't even like the place I'm living. I just need a total makeover!"

"Well, you're going to get one!" I replied. "At the rapture every believer will get a total makeover: a glorified body and a brand-new home."

At the time of the rapture, believers will be transported to the Father's house in heaven. We often talk about heaven as the Father's house, yet most of us know very little about heaven. What will it really be like? Who will be there? What will we be doing there? In John 14:1-4, Jesus gives us some answers. He was with His disciples in the upper room on the night before His death when He said:

> "Let not your hearts be troubled. Believe in God; believe also in me. In my Father's house are many rooms. If it were not so, would I have told you that I go to prepare a place

for you? And if I go and prepare a place for you, I will come again and will take you to myself, that where I am you may be also. And you know the way to where I am going" (ESV).

Several details can be observed in this passage and its following verses: the location of the Father's house, its residents, its preparations, and its future family.

The Location of the Father's House: Heaven

Three thousand years ago, King Solomon said, God "has made everything beautiful in its time. Also He has put eternity in their hearts" (Ecclesiastes 3:11). As a result, we who are created in the "image of God" can never be satisfied with that which is less than eternal. Humans have a God-given thirst for eternity. We long for an everlasting relationship with our Creator. David Jeremiah expresses his desire like this:

> We need the comfort that comes from knowing the true biblical doctrine of heaven—that wonderful place, which has been a sign of God's love for His creation from Genesis to Revelation and is more amazing than you and I could ever imagine. At the rapture of the church, Jesus will escort believers to heaven to live with Him there forever.[1]

With this hope in mind, let's consider what heaven is like as the Father's house. God has revealed much to us in His Word about our future destination. The Bible assures us that heaven is the final goal of the Christian life where we shall live forever. Thomas Constable writes:

> The "Father's house" is heaven. This is the most obvious and simple explanation, though some commentators understood it to mean the church. However, the fourth Gospel never uses the house metaphor for the church elsewhere, and the phrase "the Father's house" occurs nowhere else in Scripture as a figure of the church. Neither can it refer to the messianic kingdom, since Jesus said He was about to go there. The messianic kingdom did not exist,

and will not exist, until Jesus returns to the earth to set it up (cf. Dan. 2:44; et al.).[2]

Some interpreters have sought to suggest elaborate scenarios of where this future Father's house may be located. However, D.A. Carson's research adequately indicates the simplest explanation is best in this case:

> The simplest explanation is best: my Father's house refers to heaven, and in heaven are many rooms, many dwelling-places. The point is not the lavishness of each apartment, but the fact that such ample provision has been made that there is more than enough space for every one of Jesus' disciples to join him in his Father's home. Besides, have they not just been encouraged to trust him (v. 1), and always found strong reason to do so? Can they not therefore be assured that if heaven were other than what he has described, he would have told them?[3]

Jesus clearly came down from heaven (John 6:38) and lives there now (Acts 1:9-11). Positionally He is seated at the Father's right hand in "heavenly places" (Ephesians 1:20).

The Residents of the Father's House: God the Father, God the Son, and God the Holy Spirit

Heaven is the location where the triune God—Father, Son, and Spirit—dwells. The Father is clearly at His eternal home. The Son came from heaven and has ascended back to the Father in heaven. The Holy Spirit makes intercession for us in heaven (Romans 8:26-27). Arno Gaebelein observes:

> [H]ere in John xiv the Lord gives a new and unique revelation; He speaks of something which no prophet had promised, or even could promise. Where is it written that this Messiah would come and instead of gathering His saints into an earthly Jerusalem, would take them to the

Father's house, to the very place where He is? It is something new…a coming which concerns only His own.[4]

Of course, in addition to the Father, Son, and Spirit, the Father's house will include the heavenly angels and God's people. Far from being empty or sparse in population, the Father's house will be full. This understanding closely reflects the parable of the great supper in Luke 14 where Jesus said, "Then the master said to the servant, 'Go out into the highways and hedges, and compel them to come in, that my house may be filled'" (v. 23).

The Preparations of the Father's House: A Spacious Home

Imagine what this special place must be like. As beautiful as the earthly Paradise was in Eden, it pales in comparison to what is being prepared by the second Adam, who is the Lord from heaven. Having purchased us, He has gone ahead to prepare a place for us. The fact that He is there should attract our hearts to this amazing place.

What preparations are being made for us in our heavenly home? John MacArthur suggests:

> In ancient times, fathers had a house and their children were raised in the house. And when they got married, they built an addition on the house, and the father's house kept getting larger and larger and larger and larger and larger as apartments were built for every married child in that family, and the father's house got larger and larger and larger. And the heavenly Father's house is very large and there are many, many dwelling places.[5]

While many emphasize the importance of this heavenly home the Lord has prepared for us, it also indicates another important aspect of our lives as believers—that this world is not our true home. Jesus taught in John 17:16, "They are not of the world, just as I am not of the world." Our true home is with the Father, not in this world. Commentator Kenneth Gangel adds:

But he also wanted to indicate that he would go ahead of them to do specific work—the preparation of heaven (14:2b). The New Testament teaches us we are pilgrims and wanderers in this world. We may own homes, and some of them may be huge and beautiful. But we do not belong here because we are not primarily citizens of this world. In heaven we will be where we really belong because Jesus has gone ahead to prepare a place for us.[6]

This is why E.M. Bounds insisted that only believers could lovingly appreciate and longingly anticipate heaven. "The unconverted have no heart to sing of it for they do not know God and God does not hear them," he often said.[7]

Believers Are Citizens of the Father's House

The apostle Paul notes in Philippians 3:20, "For our citizenship is in heaven, from which we also eagerly wait for the Savior, the Lord Jesus Christ." Paul understood the importance of citizenship. Though a Jew, he also held Roman citizenship. This citizenship helped him on multiple occasions throughout his ministry. In Jerusalem, Acts 22:29 notes, "Then immediately those who were about to examine him withdrew from him; and the commander was also afraid after he found out that he was a Roman, and because he had bound him." Paul was also given permission to speak due to his Roman citizenship (Acts 21:37-40) and when necessary even to appeal directly to Caesar (Acts 25:10-12).

Peter further noted the connection between the believer and heavenly citizenship: "Beloved, I beg you as sojourners and pilgrims, abstain from fleshly lusts which war against the soul" (1 Peter 2:11). Because we do not belong to this world, we are not bound to the sin of this world. Instead, these lusts "war" against us, yet we have God's Spirit within us to provide power to prevail, just as our Lord resisted temptation in the wilderness, the garden, and at the cross.

Jesus taught that those who follow Him are literally part of a different kingdom not of this world. We belong to the kingdom of heaven. In the Sermon on the Mount, Jesus referred to the kingdom of heaven seven times (Matthew 5:3,10,19 [twice],20; 7:21; 8:11). Both John the Baptist and the disciples joined in preaching about the kingdom of heaven (Matthew 3:2; 10:7).

Elsewhere, Jesus spoke of His disciples as aliens to this world, noting, "They are not of the world, just as I am not of the world" (John 17:16). Jesus was a citizen of His Father's house in heaven. Likewise, He noted His followers were citizens of this kingdom as well. Even today, those of us who have believed in His name have become citizens of the kingdom of heaven. We live now in anticipation of our true eternal home. David Jeremiah writes:

> Just imagine the moment we get to heaven and see Jesus!
> Right now we don't see Him with our visual eyesight. The
> Bible says, "whom having not seen you love" (1 Peter 1:8)...
> If we rejoice with joy inexpressible and full of glory now,
> when we cannot see Him with visible eyesight, think of our
> joy and glory when we can![8]

A Biblical Look at Heaven

Scripture speaks often about heaven, including in twenty-three of thirty-nine Old Testament books and twenty-one of the twenty-seven New Testament books. The term *heaven* is used over five hundred times in our English Bibles. Altogether there are over seven hundred references to heaven, eternity, and the afterlife in the Bible. In the Old Testament, the Hebrew word for heaven is *shamayim*, a plural noun that literally means "the heights." In the New Testament the Greek word for heaven is *ouranos* and refers to that which is "raised up" or "lofty." In both cases the biblical concept of heaven refers to the ultimate sphere of God.

John MacArthur observes that altogether the Bible refers to three heavens: atmospheric heaven, planetary heaven, and the dwelling place of God.[9] The first heaven can be seen by day. The second heaven can be seen at night. But the third heaven can be seen only by faith.

The First Heaven

The first heaven the Bible mentions refers to the atmospheric heavens. The same words in Hebrew and Greek are used for both sky and heaven, sometimes presenting some confusion regarding which heaven is in view. For example, Psalm 19:1 reads,

> The heavens declare the glory of God;
> And the firmament shows His handiwork.

The context of this psalm clearly indicates a discussion of the sky rather than the Father's house.

Another example can be found at the flood during the time of Noah. In Genesis 7:11, we read, "On that day all the fountains of the great deep were broken up, and the windows of heaven were opened." These "windows of heaven" refer to the sky above, not the dwelling place of God. MacArthur describes it as "the troposphere—the region of breathable atmosphere that blankets the earth…where the hydrological cycle occurs."[10]

The Second Heaven

The second heaven includes the universe beyond our visible sky, including outer space, the moon, sun, and stars. This is the heaven under discussion in Genesis 1:17-18, "God set them in the firmament of the heavens to give light on the earth, and to rule over the day and over the night, and to divide the light from the darkness. And God saw that it was good."

Scripture sometimes makes this view of the heavens clear by including aspects of the second heaven within the description. In Matthew 24:29, Jesus spoke of the future when "immediately after the tribulation of those days the sun will be darkened, and the moon will not give its light; the stars will fall from heaven, and the powers of the heavens will be shaken." This heaven appears to include more than the sky, but also the region beyond that includes the stars.

The Third Heaven

The third heaven is directly mentioned by the apostle Paul in 2 Corinthians 12:2-4:

> I know a man in Christ who fourteen years ago—whether in the body I do not know, or whether out of the body I do not know, God knows—such a one was caught up to the third heaven. And I know such a man—whether in the body or out of the body I do not know, God knows—how he was caught up into Paradise and heard inexpressible words, which it is not lawful for a man to utter.

This location is equal with the Father's house or the realm of God and His angels. This heaven is referred to as "up" and as "Paradise." MacArthur explains:

> So heaven is not confined to one locality marked off by visible or measurable boundaries. It transcends the confines of time-space dimensions. Perhaps that is part of what Scripture means when it states that God inhabits eternity (Isaiah 57:15). His dwelling place—heaven—is not subject to the normal limitations of finite dimensions. We don't need to speculate about how this can be; we can simply note that this is how Scripture describes heaven. It is a real place where people with physical bodies will dwell in God's presence for all eternity, and it is also a realm that surpasses our finite concept of what a "place" is.[11]

This heaven exists in some type of unique spiritual reality unseen by human eyes or telescopes, yet has been revealed to the writers of Scripture in visions to offer us a small glimpse of what awaits those who believe. The third heaven, as Paul called it, may exist in another dimension or in the vast "supervoid" which is 1.8 billion light years across. Thomas Ice notes:

> Heaven is more than a mystical notion, imaginary dreamland, or philosophical concept. It is a real and present place

in which God, the Creator of all things lives. It is a place spoken of throughout the Bible. It is the true home of all Christians. It is where Jesus came from at the incarnation, where He ascended after the resurrection, and from whence He will come again to receive all those who truly follow Him. It is the place which the writer of Hebrews calls a "distant country" and for which those in his "hall of faith" longed (Heb. 11:13-16).[12]

Longing for Heaven

Scripture reveals three important aspects about heaven we are to look forward to as believers. These truths should lead us to long for heaven as our true home with the Lord.

Heavenly Reservations

Jesus promises that every believer has his or her name listed in the Lamb's Book of Life: "Nevertheless do not rejoice in this, that the spirits are subject to you, but rather rejoice because your names are written in heaven" (Luke 10:20). This reservation is far more important than a reservation at any restaurant or hotel. This reservation should cause us to rejoice daily as we anticipate our eternal home.

In the new heavens and earth, Revelation 21:27 declares, "But there shall by no means enter it anything that defiles, or causes an abomination or a lie, but only those who are written in the Lamb's Book of Life." Paul also notes this Book of Life in Philippians 4:3, "And I urge you also, true companion, help these women who labored with me in the gospel, with Clement also, and the rest of my fellow workers, whose names are in the Book of Life." Every believer's name is in the Book of Life. Revelation refers to this book on seven occasions, noting its importance regarding the certainty of our citizenship in heaven as believers.

Special Treatment: The Book of Life in Revelation	
3:5:	"He who overcomes shall be clothed in white garments, and I will not blot out his name from the Book of Life."
13:8:	"All who dwell on the earth will worship him, whose names have not been written in the Book of Life of the Lamb slain from the foundation of the world."
17:8:	"And those who dwell on the earth will marvel, whose names are not written in the Book of Life from the foundation of the world."
20:12:	"And I saw the dead, small and great, standing before God, and books were opened. And another book was opened, which is the Book of Life. And the dead were judged according to their works, by the things which were written in the books."
20:15:	"And anyone not found written in the Book of Life was cast into the lake of fire."
21:27:	"But there shall by no means enter it anything that defiles, or causes an abomination or a lie, but only those who are written in the Lamb's Book of Life."
22:19:	"And if anyone takes away from the words of the book of this prophecy, God shall take away his part from the Book of Life, from the holy city, and from the things which are written in this book."

Heavenly Rewards

In the Sermon on the Mount, Jesus taught, "Rejoice and be exceedingly glad, for great is your reward in heaven, for so they persecuted the prophets who were before you" (Matthew 5:12). We speak in more detail elsewhere regarding the rewards of heavenly crowns, yet Scripture often notes the importance of eternal rewards.

Jesus also condemns those who focus on rewards in this life rather than in heaven. He taught, "Take heed that you do not do your charitable deeds before men, to be seen by them. Otherwise you have no reward from your Father in heaven" (Matthew 6:1). Matthew 5:46 also reminds us, "For if you love those who love you, what reward have you? Do not even the tax collectors do the same?" The clear indication of these statements points to our eternal rewards in heaven.

Heavenly Riches

The same sermon addresses something more specific than rewards; Jesus even notes eternal riches. Matthew 6:19-21 notes:

> "Do not lay up for yourselves treasures on earth, where moth and rust destroy and where thieves break in and steal; but lay up for yourselves treasures in heaven, where neither moth nor rust destroys and where thieves do not break in and steal. For where your treasure is, there your heart will be also."

Those who invest in earthly riches over heavenly riches will ultimately regret it. In James 4:13-14, we are told,

> Come now, you who say, "Today or tomorrow we will go to such and such a city, spend a year there, buy and sell, and make a profit"; whereas you do not know what will happen tomorrow. For what is your life? It is even a vapor that appears for a little time and then vanishes away.

God has blessed us to bless others. When we do, we store up treasures in heaven rather than earthly wealth that will not last.

Seven Biblical Teachings About the Father's House

What does the Bible teach about heaven, our Father's house? Jesus told a story about Lazarus and the rich man in Luke 16:19-31 that presents seven important biblical teachings about heaven.

1. Celebration in Heaven

Lazarus was experiencing what the psalmist said, "Whom have I in heaven but You?" (Psalm 73:25). Jesus promised, "Blessed are you who weep now, for you shall laugh" (Luke 6:21.) Jesus said, "So it was that the beggar died, and was carried by the angels to Abraham's bosom" (Luke 16:22). There is no doubt where Lazarus traveled into the presence of God after death. He was with God in heaven.

While there are different views of the meaning of "Abraham's bosom" as an intermediate holding place for believers prior to the resurrection of Christ, the Bible seems to indicate that it is the same place as Paradise, which Paul equated with the third heaven (2 Corinthians 12:4).

CompellingTruth.org explains:

> One clear observation is that Abraham's side is where Abraham now lives. When Jesus referred to Abraham, He was giving His audience the highest example of a person they would know was in heaven. In Matthew 22:31-32 Jesus taught, "And as for the resurrection of the dead, have you not read what was said to you by God: 'I am the God of Abraham, and the God of Isaac, and the God of Jacob'? He is not God of the dead, but of the living." Jesus was clear Abraham was in heaven with God. Being with Abraham was a clear indication that a person was in heaven.[13]

Another way to look at this issue is to ask, "Where would Lazarus go where Abraham and angels would also dwell?" The answer is obvious—heaven! Abraham was a friend of God. Angels dwell in the presence of God. Noting Lazarus as being among them clearly indicated Lazarus was with God in heaven reclining at a banquet table in a celebration of glory next to Abraham.

2. Instantaneous Transition

Another important insight is the time involved between the end of this life and entering the presence of God. Jesus described this transition as instantaneous. There was no gap in time between the death of Lazarus and his continuing his eternal life in the presence of the Lord. There was no intermediate transition, such as purgatory.

The apostle Paul described a similar view in 2 Corinthians 5:8: "We are confident, yes, well pleased rather to be absent from the body and to be present with the Lord." Paul did not mention a waiting period, purgatory, or soul sleep, as some have erroneously taught. Instead, believers close their eyes in this life to be with the Lord in the next. Rhodes comments, "The moment a Christian dies, then, he or she is immediately with Christ in heaven. We are not just in the presence of the Lord, we are intimately present with the Lord."[14]

Psalm 23 also offers a key insight on this passage. Verse 6 says,

> Surely goodness and mercy shall follow me
> All the days of my life;
> And I will dwell in the house of the LORD
> Forever.

The psalmist declares he will follow God in this life and directly continue to live with Him for eternity in the next life.

A related important passage can be found in Luke 23:43. When the thief on the cross asked Jesus to remember him in His kingdom, Jesus answered, "Assuredly, I say to you, today you will be with Me in Paradise." This man had no opportunity to live a changed life or even to be baptized. However, Jesus accepted the man's simple, sincere faith and assured him of eternity in heaven *that day*.

3. Fellowship with Believers

A third observation from Jesus' teaching regarding Lazarus is the presence of other believers. He was taken to Abraham's bosom. He was with Abraham. If Abraham is with the Lord (Matthew 8:11), it is obvious other Old Testament believers, as well as every believer who has passed on before us, is there as well. In emphasizing life after death, Jesus referred to Abraham, Isaac, and Jacob and said: "God is not the God of the dead, but of the living" (Matthew 22:32). Elijah was caught up into heaven (2 Kings 2:1,11). Stephen, the first Christian martyr, called on the risen Christ and said, "Lord Jesus, receive my spirit" (Acts 7:59).

One of the joys we most look forward to in heaven is the ability to stand reunited with our loved ones who have gone before us. Our parents, siblings, family members, and friends who are now in

God's presence will be with us once again. In commenting on this Billy Graham said:

> Yes, I have every confidence that we will be reunited with our loved ones who have gone to Heaven before us. Heaven is a place of perfect happiness—and one of its greatest joys will be our reunion with those we love. God loves us, and He will not withhold that joy from us![15]

This also serves as the basis for addressing the issue of whether infants and young children who have passed away will join us again in heaven. I am convinced they will. In 2 Samuel 12:23, David's infant son died. When he heard the tragic news, David noted, "I shall go to him." This was not a reference only to going to the grave, but to a positive future where all wrongs will be made right, and we will be reunited with our beloved infants and young children who have passed away before us.

Further, the transfiguration (Matthew 17:1-9) shows we will be able to recognize one another in heaven. Moses and Elijah did not lose their identities, nor did they exist in a bodiless form. Instead, they could be recognized by the Lord as well as by Peter, James, and John. Even Jesus, though unique as the Lord, was recognized in His resurrected body. Puritan minister Richard Baxter wrote:

> The Christian will not be so singular as to be solitary. Though heaven is proper to the saints only, yet is it common to all the saints, for what it is but an association of blessed spirits in God; a corporation of perfected saints, whereof Christ is the head; the communion of saints completed?[16]

4. Joyful Experience

Luke 16:25 notes Abraham answering the rich man in his agony, saying, "Son, remember that in your lifetime you received your good things, and likewise Lazarus evil things; but now he is comforted and you are tormented." This emphasis on "good things" highlights heaven will not be a mundane world in which we robotically bow before God. Instead, we will experience the full presence of the Lord, His angels, His people, and all the good things of God.

One chapter earlier, Luke twice mentions joy in heaven. Luke 15:7 states, "I say to you that likewise there will be more joy in heaven over one sinner who repents than over ninety-nine just persons who need no repentance." Luke 15:10 adds, "Likewise, I say to you, there is joy in the presence of the angels of God over one sinner who repents."

Heaven will not only include joy in the future; there is much joy there now. Joy is heightened among the angels every time a new person comes to faith in Jesus. If this is the joy that takes place over the answered prayers of one sinner turning to Jesus, just imagine the joy spread throughout the Father's house. We need not worry about whether heaven will be fun. We will enjoy every moment in the Lord's presence more than we could ever imagine.

5. Blissful Comfort

Luke 16:25 also highlights the comfort we will experience in heaven: "He is comforted and you are tormented." The rich man endured suffering. Lazarus experienced comfort. In addition to the joy of the good things in heaven, we will enjoy relief from the discomforts and misfortunes of this life.

These words are especially powerful for believers who have endured much suffering in this life. Many Christians live in poverty or under intense persecution. They have been rejected by family and friends, opposed by coworkers, or scorned by their own leaders. Yet one day this discomfort will be replaced with the perfect comfort of living with the heavenly Father, enjoying perfect fellowship with Him and His children.

6. Eternal Memories

Jesus also notes an important insight regarding our memories in heaven. Verse 25 uses the phrase, "Son, remember that in your lifetime…" This mention of remembering affirms the Bible's teaching elsewhere that we will still have our memories in heaven. For example, 1 Corinthians 13:12 notes, "Now I know in part, but then I shall know just as I also am known." We will know more in heaven, not less. In fact, once we are in our final glorified state in heaven, we will understand everything from God's perspective.

W.A. Criswell taught, "I'll be the same person then that I am now—only with all the imperfections and limitations of sin finally removed. This is a wonderful thought—that the essence of who we are will remain throughout eternity—yet vastly improved by God's grace."[17] In addition, there is at least one mention in Scripture of people who will remember earthly events while in heaven. Revelation 6:10-11 states:

> And they cried with a loud voice, saying, "How long, O Lord, holy and true, until You judge and avenge our blood on those who dwell on the earth?" Then a white robe was given to each of them; and it was said to them that they should rest a little while longer, until both the number of their fellow servants and their brethren, who would be killed as they were, was completed.

These believers appear to be those who come to faith in Jesus during the tribulation and are then martyred and live in God's presence. Though they will experience pain on earth, they are comforted in heaven. Still, they will retain the memories of their past. In a similar way, we will retain our earthly memories in heaven, yet in a redeemed manner that sees God's full providential work in every aspect of our lives.

7. Eternal State

The last aspect Jesus emphasizes in the passage of Lazarus and the rich man is eternity. Luke 16:26 says, "And besides all this, between us and you there is a great gulf fixed, so that those who want to pass from here to you cannot, nor can those from there pass to us." Once this life ends, we will no longer be able to make any decisions that will move us from hell to heaven or heaven to hell. There are only two options, with no purgatory or limbo where we temporarily endure suffering for past sins. Instead, our decision regarding whether to trust in Christ as Savior in this life will determine our eternal destiny in the next life.

Frequently Asked Questions About Heaven

Many additional questions about heaven also exist. The following six questions are commonly noted.

Who Are the Great Cloud of Witnesses?

Hebrews 12:1 mentions a "great cloud of witnesses" in heaven. The verse notes we are "surrounded" by them. Who are the witnesses in this group and what is their role in our lives today?

The larger context of Hebrews 11–12 discusses what is often referred to as the hall of faith or faith hall of fame and includes biblical leaders such as Enoch, Abel, Noah, Abraham, and others. Their faithful lives and activities are noted as examples for us today. This great cloud of witnesses includes those named in the list of Hebrews 11, but also includes much more. Hebrews 11:32 explains, "And what more shall I say? For the time would fail me to tell of Gideon and Barak and Samson and Jephthah, also of David and Samuel and the prophets." The author of Hebrews certainly includes the godly leaders of the Old Testament writings in this group.

In addition, verses 35-38 refer to events beyond those listed in the Old Testament. These may include early Christian believers persecuted near the time Hebrews was written. Some even suggest one reason Hebrews was written anonymously was due to the harsh persecution taking place in Rome toward Christians during this time (approximately AD 64–68 under Emperor Nero).

Hebrews 11:39-40 summarizes the activities of the entire group, stating, "And all these, having obtained a good testimony through faith, did not receive the promise, God having provided something better for us, that they should not be made perfect apart from us." The phrase "all these" appears to include all past believers in heaven as part of this great cloud of witnesses.

Others take the concept a step further and argue those in heaven can somehow see what we are doing today. Though not all interpreters agree with this view, this passage appears to point toward the possibility of our heavenly forerunners observing our actions. If angels can see what is taking place (1 Corinthians 4:9) and examples can be observed elsewhere of Samuel (1 Samuel 28:3-20) and Moses and Elijah (Luke 9:28-31), why would this not be true of other believers? Even Revelation 19:1-6 expresses a conversation in heaven where believers are aware of Babylon's fall on earth. In addition, Isaiah 66:22-24 indicates those in heaven will see the destruction of the lost.

However, we do not need the watchful eyes of believers in heaven to provide additional accountability to live for God while in this world. Instead, we have the teachings of God's faithful leaders in Scripture as well as the indwelling ministry of the Holy Spirit to guide us. These past believers can serve as faithful examples to us, as Hebrews 11 emphasizes, rather than existing as hovering spirits who watch our daily actions. We are called to give an account to the Lord, not to heavenly saints (1 Corinthians 3:10-15).

In either case, the application is clear: The author used the faithful actions of past believers to encourage the faithful actions of present believers. Hebrews 12:1-2 encourages, "Let us lay aside every weight, and the sin which so easily ensnares us, and let us run with endurance the race that is set before us, looking unto Jesus, the author and finisher of our faith." Despite trials, we can look to the example of Jesus and His followers who have gone before us for inspiration to continue serving the Lord today.

Do People Become Angels in Heaven?

Our culture has popularized the concept that people become angels in heaven. The idea of humans taking on wings and floating upon clouds has become prevalent in many movies and songs. This has especially been noted during tragic events when young children die, with loved ones claiming, "God has another angel in heaven."

While not attempting to be insensitive to those who have lost loved ones, the Bible nowhere expresses the idea that people become angels in heaven. Instead, unbelievers are eternally separated from the Lord, while believers instantly enter the presence of the Lord. While believers will receive a new body at the time of the rapture, we must also continue to exist in some sort of bodily existence while in heaven.

For example, Moses and Elijah were clearly identifiable in heavenly bodies at the transfiguration. The resurrected Jesus was identified by His friends. In heaven, we will appear among all believers who have gone before us, including our saved loved ones, recognizing one another and living among the angels in heaven as we worship the Lord. However, there is no indication we will turn into angels, despite living among them.

What Are the Angels Like in Heaven?

Scripture often speaks of angels, both in heaven as well as serving God's purposes on earth. Heaven will include "thousands upon thousands" of angels (Daniel 7:9-10; Hebrews 12:22) who exist to praise the Lord (Isaiah 6:1-6). Revelation 5:11-12 offers a look at the heavenly activities of angelic beings. They praise the Lord, honoring Him with "a loud voice."

Activities of heavenly angels in addition to praising God include:

- protecting (Psalm 91:11-12)
- providing (1 Kings 19:5-8; Matthew 4:1-11)
- proclaiming (Luke 1:8-20; Revelation 14:6-11)
- punishing (Revelation 12:7-9)

Charles Ryrie further notes the Bible's attention to the superior knowledge of angels in heaven:

> (1) Angels were created as a higher order of creatures in the universe than humans are. Therefore, innately they possess greater knowledge. (2) Angels study the Bible more thoroughly than some humans do and gain knowledge from it (James 2:19; Rev. 12:12). (3) Angels gain

knowledge through long observation of human activities. Unlike humans, angels do not have to study the past; they have experienced it. Therefore, they know how others have acted and reacted in situations and can predict with a greater degree of accuracy how we may act in similar circumstances. The experiences of longevity give them greater knowledge.[18]

Will There Be Animals or Pets in Heaven?

It has become very popular in our culture to believe all animals and pets go to heaven. A close look at Scripture shows an unresolved conclusion to this issue. It is clear there will be animals in heaven. For example, Revelation speaks of various horses involved in God's judgments, while heavenly horses of fire took Elijah to heaven (2 Kings 2:11-12).

Further, God certainly cares deeply for animal life. He created all living things (Genesis 1). Jesus said not a single sparrow is forgotten before the Lord (Luke 12:6-7). However, when we look at the issue of pets, we are not given an indication that the animals we care about on earth will be the same animals we will find in heaven. Scripture makes a distinction between humans made in the image of God (Genesis 1:26-27) and the creation of animal life, which is not eternal. Animals exist for our earthly enjoyment. Presumably there will continue to be animals in heaven that serve God's purposes. Beyond that, we must await heaven to discover the complete answer. As Paul writes,

> "Eye has not seen, nor ear heard,
> Nor have entered into the heart of man
> The things which God has prepared for those who love
> Him."
>
> (1 Corinthians 2:9)

How Many People Will Be in Heaven?

The Bible does not provide the exact number of people who will be in heaven. However, we do find some indications. First, Jesus taught, "Because narrow is the gate and difficult is the way which leads to life, and there are few who find it" (Matthew 7:14). This would seem to point toward a view in which fewer people will enter heaven than we might initially expect. However, other Scriptures emphasize the vast number of people in heaven. For example, Revelation 7 and 14 speak of 144,000 male Jews who will believe in Jesus just in the seven-year tribulation period. They will serve as evangelists, reaching many others during this time for Christ.

After the report of these 144,000 Jews, Revelation 7:9-10 states:

> After these things I looked, and behold, a great multitude which no one could number, of all nations, tribes, peoples, and tongues, standing before the throne and before the Lamb, clothed with white robes, with palm branches in their hands, and crying out with a loud voice, saying, "Salvation belongs to our God who sits on the throne, and to the Lamb!"

The number of people in heaven will be a number "no one could count." Revelation 5:9 adds the twenty-four elders praising Jesus with the words,

> "You are worthy to take the scroll,
> And to open its seals;
> For You were slain,
> And have redeemed us to God by Your blood
> Out of every tribe and tongue and people and nation."

People from every people group will live among the redeemed.

John Hart observes: "For all eternity, heaven will be a continuing experience of new adventures that will bring us into community and unbroken friendships with others…They will become like intimate family or best friends."[19]

How You Can Prepare for the Father's House

Jesus is preparing a home for us in heaven. How are we to prepare for our meeting with Him? Arthur Pink describes one important way we can prepare for our heavenly dwelling—living with eager anticipation:

> Today the average "home" is little more than a boarding-house—a place to eat and sleep in. But "home" used to mean, and still means to a few, the place where we are loved for our own sakes; the place where we are always welcome; the place whither we can retire from the strife of the world and enjoy rest and peace, the place where loved ones are together. Such will Heaven be. Believers are now in a strange country, yea, in an enemy's land; in the life to come, they will be at *Home!*[20]

God provides many insights into our future life in the Father's house. Yet many of us fail to see the next life as better than what we enjoy today. Perhaps Erwin Lutzer described it best when he wrote, "The fact that we don't view death with optimism just might be because we think of death as taking us from our home rather than bringing us to our home! Unlike Paul, we have become so attached to our tent that we just don't want to move."[21]

This is especially true in an age of materialism, prosperity, and success. We have much to hold us to earth. As a result, we often lose sight of our eternal destination. It is not that we resist heaven because of the appeal of hell but because of the love of earth. This is why the Bible reminds us that the things of this world alone will never satisfy the deepest longings of the human heart. We were made for something better than this! That is why Charles Wesley wrote: "Our conflicts here shall soon be past, when you and I ascend at last."[22]

4

THE JUDGMENT SEAT OF CHRIST: OUR HEAVENLY REWARDS

What will happen after the rapture to the Father's house? The next prophetic event will be Christ's judgment seat in heaven. This judgment will include all believers from the church age between the Day of Pentecost and the rapture. We will individually receive rewards based on our ministry to the Lord. To be clear, this is only one of seven future judgments predicted in Scripture. The full list of future judgments will include:

1. The judgment seat of Christ (2 Corinthians 5:10)

2. The judgment of Old Testament believers after the second coming (Daniel 12:1-3)

3. The judgment of tribulation believers (Revelation 20:4-6)

4. The judgment of Jews at the second coming (Ezekiel 20:33-38)

5. The judgment of Gentiles at the second coming (Matthew 25:31-46)

6. The judgment of Satan and demons (Revelation 20:10)

7. The judgment of the great white throne (Revelation 20:11-15)

One of the many blessings of trusting in Jesus now is that we will face only one judgment—the judgment seat of Christ. This judgment will not determine whether we enter heaven, but it will determine our rewards in eternity. How you live your life as a believer today will determine how God blesses your life for eternity.

Woodrow Kroll writes: "God is the one who developed the rewards, determined the criteria for awarding them, and demonstrated his grace by providing them for faithful service. Rewards arise from the heart of God."[1] Mark Hitchcock adds this thought: "According to the Bible, the all-knowing, all-seeing God is keeping track of how you're living and what you're doing for Him every day...Rewards for serving Christ faithfully are beyond our wildest imagination."[2]

When: The Time of the Judgment Seat

When will the judgment seat of Christ take place? First Corinthians 4:5 notes, "Therefore judge nothing before the time, until the Lord comes, who will both bring to light the hidden things of darkness and reveal the counsels of the hearts. Then each one's praise will come from God." When will the Lord come? At the rapture (1 Thessalonians 4:13-18). Dwight Pentecost adds, "In 1 Corinthians 4:5; 2 Timothy 4:8; and Revelation 22:12 the reward is associated with 'that day,' that is, the day in which He comes for His own. Thus it must be observed that the rewarding of the church must take place between the rapture and the revelation of Christ to the earth."[3]

Interestingly, this judgment will include both the positive and the negative actions and attitudes we have toward the Lord. This detail serves as a powerful reminder that how we live now matters for eternity. Yes, Jesus forgives every sin. However, I do not want to stand before the Lord and know there were ways I could have lived differently by more fully yielding to the Spirit of God at work in me. We should live highly motivated to serve the Lord with all our heart, soul, and mind (Matthew 22:34-40), knowing our lives at this moment matter forever.

Where: The Location of the Judgment Seat

If the judgment seat of Christ takes place after the rapture, it will not occur on earth. The most likely location will be heaven. Why? Our judgment will take place before the Lord's "seat." The Lord will be in heaven, meaning our judgment will take place there as well. "For we must all appear before the judgment seat of Christ, that each one may receive the things done in the body, according to what he has done, whether good or bad" (2 Corinthians 5:10). This "judgment seat" is a translation of the Greek word *bema*.

What is this bema seat? Don Stewart writes: "The bema is a tribunal for rewards. In the large Olympic arenas, there was an elevated seat on which the judge of the contest sat. After the contests were over, the successful competitors would assemble before the bema to receive their rewards or crowns."[4] In fact, the word *bema* was "taken from Isthmian games where the contestants would compete for the prize under the careful scrutiny of judges who would make sure that every rule of the contest was obeyed (2 Timothy 2:5). The victor of a given event who participated according to the rules was led by the judge to the platform called the *Bema*. There the laurel wreath was placed on his head as a symbol of victory (1 Corinthians 9:24-25)."[5] John MacArthur adds in his commentary on 2 Corinthians 5:10:

> Judgment seat translates *bema*, which, in its simplest definition, describes a place reached by steps, or a platform. The Septuagint (the Greek translation of the Old Testament) uses it that way in Nehemiah 8:4. In Greek culture *bema* referred to the elevated platform on which victorious athletes received their crowns, much like the medal stand in the modern Olympic games. In the New Testament it was used on the judgment seats of Pilate (Matt. 27:19; John 19:13), Herod (Acts 12:21), and Festus (Acts 25:6,10,17). There was also a *bema* at Corinth, where unbelieving Jews unsuccessfully accused Paul before the Roman proconsul Gallio (Acts 18:12,16,17). A person was brought before a *bema* to have his or her deeds examined, in a judicial sense

for indictment or exoneration, or for the purpose of recognizing and rewarding some achievement. Writing to the
Romans of this same event, Paul described it as "the judgment seat [*bema*] of God" (Rom 14:10). God the Father is
the ultimate Judge, but He has "given all judgment to the
Son" (John 5:22).[6]

This judgment seat will serve as the appropriate location for the righteous Judge to conduct His review and rewards of church-age believers.

Who: The People of the Judgment

The bema seat judgment is for believers. Every follower of Jesus
taken up at the rapture will be included. This stands in contrast with
unbelievers who will later be judged at the great white throne judgment
for condemnation (Revelation 20:11-15). At the bema seat, church-age
believers must all be judged (2 Corinthians 5:10).

According to this verse, every believer will be judged regarding
"the things done in the body, according to what he has done." This
evaluation will serve as an examination of our actions as believers.
Hitchcock adds:

> The people at this judgment will be believers only. The con-
> text of 2 Corinthians 5:10 indicates that "we" refers to Paul
> and other believers. The purpose of the judgment seat of
> Christ is not to determine if a person is admitted to heaven
> or not. The purpose of the judgment seat of Christ is two-
> fold: to review and to reward. The Lord will review our
> conduct (Rom 14:10-12), service (1 Cor 3:13), words (Matt
> 12:36), thoughts, and motives (1 Corinthians 4:5) after we
> became a believer in Christ. Based on this review we will
> receive rewards from our gracious Lord.[7]

Jesus Christ Himself will be the judge. Pentecost explains:

> 2 Corinthians 5:10 makes it clear that this examination is
> conducted before the presence of the Son of God. John
> 5:22 states that all judgment has been committed into the

hand of the Son. The fact that this same event is referred to in Romans 14:10 as "the judgment seat of God" would indicate that God has committed this judgment into the hand of the Son also. A part of the exaltation of Christ is the right to manifest divine authority in judgment.[8]

The participants of this judgment will involve the perfect Son of God and the redeemed of the Lord. We will stand before Him as He provides His perfect evaluation of our lives on earth.

Why: The Purpose of the Judgment

The bema seat judgment does not determine heaven or hell. We already will be in heaven when this judgment takes place. Instead, the purpose of this judgment will determine rewards among God's people. We are saved by grace alone through faith alone in Christ alone (Ephesians 2:8-9). However, we are also created to complete works given to us by our Father (Ephesians 2:10). The bema seat will stand as an evaluation of how faithfully we have accomplished God's plan for our life, not how we compare against anyone else. Paul describes this evaluation as a purifying fire:

> Now if anyone builds on this foundation with gold, silver, precious stones, wood, hay, straw, each one's work will become clear; for the Day will declare it, because it will be revealed by fire; and the fire will test each one's work, of what sort it is. If anyone's work which he has built on it endures, he will receive a reward. If anyone's work is burned, he will suffer loss; but he himself will be saved, yet so as through fire (1 Corinthians 3:12-15).

Our rewards will be based on what we have built upon the foundation of Jesus Christ. Our human efforts or abilities are not the focus. Neither will the Lord use other people as our standard of comparison. The godly servant often overlooked in this life may serve as one of the most rewarded in the next. Jesus taught in Mark 9:35, "If anyone desires to be first, he shall be last of all and servant of all." Despite the legendary spiritual status of Moses, his reputation was built upon a lifestyle of service rather than upon his human abilities: "And Moses indeed was faithful in all His house as a servant" (Hebrews 3:5). Lewis Sperry Chafer and John Walvoord write we will not be judged regarding works for salvation but rather our actions as believers:

> With reference to sin, Scripture teaches that the child of God under grace shall not come into judgment (John 3:18; 5:24; 6:37; Rom. 5:1; 8:1; 1 Cor. 11:32); in his standing before God, and on the ground that the penalty for all sin—past, present, and future (Col. 2:13)—has been borne by Christ as the perfect Substitute, the believer is not only placed beyond condemnation, but being in Christ is accepted in the perfection of Christ (1 Cor. 1:30; Eph. 1:6; Col. 2:10; Heb. 10:14) and loved of God as Christ is loved (John 17:23).[9]

Jesus also spoke of rewards in the Sermon on the Mount. Matthew 6 notes three occasions in which He taught that those who are hypocrites and seek only the praise of people "have their reward" (vv. 2,5,16). Verse 1 says, "Take heed that you do not do your charitable deeds before men, to be seen by them. Otherwise you have no reward from your Father in heaven." The word translated "reward" is used a total of seven times in this chapter. The final time is found verse 18, where Jesus clearly states, "Your Father who sees in secret will reward you openly."

How: The Method of the Judgment

We've discussed the when, where, and why of the bema seat, but how will this judgment take place? Scripture offers several concepts to help us better understand the ways our Lord will evaluate our service on that day.

First, Christ will judge without favoritism. Even the opponents of Jesus recognized, "You do not show personal favoritism" (Luke 20:21). In Galatians 2:6, Paul directly adds, "God shows personal favoritism to no man." Romans 2:11 further emphasizes, "For there is no partiality with God," while Colossians 3:25 notes, "But he who does wrong will be repaid for what he has done, and there is no partiality."

Second, Christ will judge fairly. Were you born into poverty? God knows and will perfectly take this into account. Did you experience a difficult upbringing or family situation? He knows. Were you limited by physical problems, a struggling financial issue, or lived in a location filled with problems? Good news! The Lord judges fairly. As Lehman Strauss notes, "Believers never need fear a condemnatory judgment for sin. For every Christian this judgment is already past. When Jesus comes again He will have in His body the marks of crucifixion, and this will prove that the penalty for sin has been paid in full."[10]

The people of Israel had accused the Lord of not judging fairly. Ezekiel 33:20 provides God's response: "Yet you say, 'The way of the Lord is not fair.' O house of Israel, I will judge every one of you according to his own ways." God doesn't need our excuses or explanations. He sees everything and knows our situation perfectly. We can trust He will perfectly evaluate our situation and personal background to judge according to His standards.

Third, Christ will judge personally. We must "all appear" (2 Corinthians 5:10) and "each of us shall give account of himself to God" (Romans 14:12). This call is for every believer, yet for each one of us to also individually receive rewards from our Savior. Romans 2:6 adds, God "will render to each one according to his deeds."

These three factors encourage us to focus on eternity rather than on the temporary. Jesus further taught in Matthew 6:19-21:

> "Do not lay up for yourselves treasures on earth, where moth and rust destroy and where thieves break in and steal; but lay up for yourselves treasures in heaven, where neither moth nor rust destroys and where thieves do not break in and steal. For where your treasure is, there your heart will be also."

Our Lord longs for us to concentrate our lives on treasures in heaven that He will one day personally give us. If we are faithfully living for what matters most, we need not fear this future judgment, but can look forward to it with anticipation. Like the apostle John's final plea in Revelation 22:20, we can cry out, "Come, Lord Jesus!"

What: The Aspects of the Judgment

Finally, let's consider what our Lord will judge at the bema seat. As the perfect judge, His standard of evaluation is all that will matter on that day.

First, the Lord will judge us according to the truth we have received. Luke 12:48 teaches, "But he who did not know, yet committed things deserving of stripes, shall be beaten with few. For everyone to whom much is given, from him much will be required; and to whom much has been committed, of him they will ask the more." A person living in an illiterate society with little access to Scripture or other resources will not be treated the same as those of us who have endless Bible resources in the palm of our hand on smartphones.

Further, Scripture notes church leaders will be judged more strictly because of their role. James 3:1 reminds us, "My brethren, let not many of you become teachers, knowing that we shall receive a stricter judgment." Those most familiar with God's truth should be expected to best reflect His truth.

Second, the Lord will judge us according to our works. In Jesus' letters to the seven churches of Revelation, it is interesting to note the end of Revelation 2:23: "I will give to each one of you according to your works." Jesus concludes this final book of Scripture by reaffirming, "And behold, I am coming quickly, and My reward is with Me, to give to every one according to his work" (Revelation 22:12). In the Old Testament, the Lord spoke through Jeremiah, stating,

> "I, the LORD, search the heart,
> I test the mind,
> Even to give every man according to his ways,
> According to the fruit of his doings."
> (Jeremiah 17:10)

Erwin Lutzer writes, "Although we must admit that many so-called Christians are not Christians at all, we also must recognize that serious failure is possible for genuine Christians. And this will be revealed at the *Bema*."[11]

Third, the Lord will judge us according to our abilities. Every believer is blessed with spiritual gifts, natural talents, and even specific callings given by God. For example, Ephesians 2:10 notes, "For we are His workmanship, created in Christ Jesus for good works, which God prepared beforehand that we should walk in them." Each of us has a certain set of abilities from the Lord to serve Him and others. Moses was called to lead God's people out of slavery (Exodus 3–4). Joshua led the same group of people but was given a unique calling to bring God's people into the promised land.

The Lord called Jeremiah to be a prophet. Jeremiah claimed he was too young and did not know how to speak, yet God focused on His calling to equip Jeremiah for his work (Jeremiah 1:4-19). Scripture frequently notes such calling passages in the lives of leaders such as Abraham, Moses, Samuel, and others, affirming His calling as an important aspect of how He will evaluate our lives in eternity.

Jonah initially resisted the call of God to speak to the people of Nineveh. Yet the Lord changed Jonah's situation, leading Jonah to repent in prayer (Jonah 2) and later answer God's unique call upon his life. Even when we initially fail in this life, God often provides second chances to fulfill His destiny for us.

Fourth, the Lord will judge us according to our faithfulness. In the parable of the talents (referring to a unit of money, not natural abilities), Jesus emphasized the importance of faithful living as part of His standard of evaluation: "Well done, good and faithful servant; you were faithful over a few things, I will make you ruler over many things. Enter into the joy of your lord" (Matthew 25:21,23; Luke 19:17). Faithfulness can also sometimes include enduring suffering or hardship for serving Christ. Persecution tests our faithfulness, yet also results in blessing. One of the crowns given by our Lord is based on suffering for the faith.

Fifth, the Lord will judge us according to the standard of Christ. Jesus taught, "Also I say to you, whoever confesses Me before men, him the Son of Man also will confess before the angels of God. But he who denies Me before men will be denied before the angels of God" (Luke 12:8-9). Again, we will not be compared with the works or abilities of others. We will not find ourselves evaluated by the standards of this world. All that will matter is how we have served based on the teachings and revelation of Jesus Christ.

What will receiving rewards feel like in heaven? Will we regret lost rewards or sense remorse for the ways we failed the Lord on earth? Samuel Hoyt compares this judgment to a graduation ceremony, offering these encouraging words:

> The judgment seat of Christ might be compared to a commencement ceremony. At graduation there is some measure of disappointment and remorse that one did not do better and work harder. However, at such an event the overwhelming emotion is joy, not remorse. The graduates do not leave the auditorium weeping because they did not earn better grades. Rather, they are thankful that they have been graduated, and they are grateful for what they did achieve. To overdo the sorrow aspect of the judgment seat of Christ is to make heaven hell. To underdo the sorrow aspect is to make faithfulness inconsequential.[12]

Our Rewards: The Crowns of Eternity

The Bible doesn't provide every detail about our future rewards in heaven. However, it does mention five types of crowns that can be received for faithful service to the Lord. These crowns are not the golden adornments of a king or queen like we imagine but are based on the Greco-Roman tradition of crown wreaths used in ancient competitions. They served as a symbol of accomplishment rather than as an item of great wealth, noting the important achievement reached through a hard-fought victory. The crowns Scripture mentions include:

Crown 1: The Imperishable Crown

The imperishable crown will be given to those who exhibit faithful endurance through trials: "Do you not know that those who run in a race all run, but one receives the prize? Run in such a way that you may obtain it. And everyone who competes for the prize is temperate in all things. Now they do it to obtain a perishable crown, but we for an imperishable crown" (1 Corinthians 9:24-25).

Paul uses a running analogy. Many run but not everyone will receive a prize. What did Paul stress as important for those who desire to receive this imperishable crown from our Lord? He spoke of the need to be temperate in all things. To win in a race involves a tremendous amount of discipline. Early mornings and long days were (and are) part of the daily rigor of the athlete who seeks to succeed at the highest levels. If we desire to receive this crown, the method is clear—we must remain focused on the works of our Father in heaven.

Crown 2: The Crown of Rejoicing

Paul speaks of a crown of rejoicing in 1 Thessalonians 2:19: "For what is our hope, or joy, or crown of rejoicing? Is it not even you in the presence of our Lord Jesus Christ at His coming?" In Acts 17, we read of Paul's journey to the city of Thessalonica where he reached a new group of people with the gospel and helped start a new church.

This crown is clearly associated with leading people to faith in Christ. However, David Jeremiah rightly notes this crown may not be limited only to those who directly lead other people to Christ:

> This is sometimes called the Soul Winner's Crown, but I suspect it isn't just reserved for those who actually lead another person to Christ. I think it will be shared by all those who play a role in bringing others to Christ. It's a team effort. Whenever I have the opportunity of leading others to receive Jesus as Savior, I almost always find that someone else has already planted the seed of the gospel in their hearts.[13]

Strauss adds, "Every time an individual is converted, there is joy in Heaven; but at the day of the giving of rewards the soul-winner will be exceeding joyful when those are presented to God whom he had won to Christ."[14]

Crown 3: The Crown of Righteousness

In 2 Timothy 4:8, Paul writes near the end of his life, "Finally, there is laid up for me the crown of righteousness, which the Lord, the righteous Judge, will give to me on that Day, and not to me only but also to all who have loved His appearing." What is this crown of righteousness? This crown is directly associated with those who "love" the appearing of the Lord. This is another important reason to long for the coming of the Lord at the rapture! Not only does this perspective lead us to live with righteousness now; it will also lead to an eternal reward in the form of the crown of righteousness. This crown will far surpass any earthly achievement. Jeremiah notes:

> At the Bema Seat of Christ, earthly wreaths and trophies and newspaper clippings and Super Bowl rings will be long forgotten. They'll be no more important than brushing your teeth or buying a newspaper at the corner store. But what we do for eternity—even the smallest of deeds—will count forever.[15]

Crown 4: The Crown of Glory

Peter specifically mentions a crown of glory for those who shepherd or lead God's people:

> Shepherd the flock of God which is among you, serving as overseers, not by compulsion but willingly, not for dishonest gain but eagerly; nor as being lords over those entrusted to you, but being examples to the flock; and when the Chief Shepherd appears, you will receive the crown of glory that does not fade away (1 Peter 5:2-5).

The expectations for receiving this crown include not only shepherding, but also willing service, avoiding dishonest gain, humility, and serving as an example to others. As Paul also notes in Romans 8:18, "For I consider that the sufferings of this present time are not worthy to be compared with the glory which shall be revealed in us."

He adds in 2 Corinthians 4:17-18, "For our light affliction, which is but for a moment, is working for us a far more exceeding and eternal weight of glory, while we do not look at the things which are seen, but at the things which are not seen. For the things which are seen are temporary, but the things which are not seen are eternal." The late John Stott notes on this topic, "The sufferings and the glory belong together indissolubly. They did in the experience of Christ; they do in the experience of his people also. It is only after we 'have suffered a little while' that we will enter God's 'eternal glory in Christ,' to which he has called us."[16]

It has been said there are many pastors but few shepherds. The church has many leaders, but too few servants who truly live out the calling required for the crown of glory. If this is the challenge for church leaders, it also serves as a goal for other believers. We must all seek to live as servant leaders who exemplify a life worthy of the calling we have received in the Lord (Ephesians 4:1).

Crown 5: The Crown of Life

James, the half-brother of the Lord Jesus Christ, served as a leader in the first church of Jerusalem and wrote one of the first letters in the New Testament. His readers were already experiencing suffering for teaching Jesus as Lord, and in James 1:12, he encouraged them with these words: "Blessed is the man who endures temptation; for when he has been approved, he will receive the crown of life which the Lord has promised to those who love Him."

Jonathan Falwell comments on this verse:

> God allows us to traverse a challenging road in this life, all the while guaranteeing that if we allow him to work in us, he will make sure we finish well. Waiting on God during trials is a rite of passage in the Christian life, and it leads to our ultimate completeness in Christ. It will do nothing but make us better for the future.[17]

What will we do with these crowns? They will not be for our glory, but for worshipping the one who gives them to us. Revelation 4:10-11 tells us that even the twenty-four elders in the Lord's presence will "cast their crowns before the throne, saying:

> "'You are worthy, O Lord,
> To receive glory and honor and power;
> For You created all things,
> And by Your will they exist and were created.'"

Regarding what more we would wish to know about these crowns, Lutzer rightly suggests:

> We do not know everything we would like to know about rewards. We simply do not understand how Christ will balance our good deeds with those that are worthless. We must be content to know that Christ will be fair and generous. Whatever He does will be acceptable; no one will question His judgment. He will meticulously separate the perishable from the imperishable.[18]

Our future crowns will certainly give us a great sense of joy. However, they will pale in comparison with the joy of living eternally in the presence of our King.

Standing Strong: Preparing for the Judgment

Scripture provides ways for us to prepare for this upcoming time of judgment. In the apostle Paul's final letter, he leaves Timothy (and us) three important analogies to help in living fully for the Lord until the moment He takes us to heaven to be with Him, whether we meet Him upon passing from this world or meet Him at the rapture. Second Timothy 2:1-7 says:

> You therefore, my son, be strong in the grace that is in Christ Jesus. And the things that you have heard from me among many witnesses, commit these to faithful men who will be able to teach others also. You therefore must endure hardship as a good soldier of Jesus Christ. No one

engaged in warfare entangles himself with the affairs of this life, that he may please him who enlisted him as a soldier. And also if anyone competes in athletics, he is not crowned unless he competes according to the rules. The hardworking farmer must be first to partake of the crops. Consider what I say, and may the Lord give you understanding in all things.

Each of these examples—a good soldier, an athlete, and a hardworking farmer—provides helpful encouragement and insight for us today.

A Good Soldier

Roman soldiers were common throughout the Roman Empire of the first century, with duties ranging from guarding political leaders to their involvement at the crucifixion of Jesus. The "good soldier" focused on two important insights that Paul notes in this passage. First, the good soldier endures hardship. Today, America's Navy Seals have a saying, "The only easy day was yesterday." Similarly, Roman soldiers regularly encountered situations far more difficult than those encountered by the everyday citizen. Whether actively engaging in battle or assessing areas for threats to safety, soldiers must remain constantly vigilant and prepared for any situation.

Second, a good soldier does not entangle himself "with the affairs of this life." While nonsoldiers can focus on entertainment or personal pursuits, soldiers do not have such luxuries. They must focus on following the commands of their leader and completing the goal of their mission. Similarly, believers are to focus on the Lord and His calling for our lives. Such living leads to eternal rewards.

An Athlete

The second reference Paul made was to an athlete. Notice the areas he emphasizes. First, an athlete competes. Winning athletes do not simply run or shoot baskets or kick goals for personal fulfilment; their emphasis is on defeating the competition. Similarly, believers are not called to selfish desires, but rather to defeating our spiritual enemies and fulfilling the Great Commission (Matthew 28:18-20).

In addition, a competitive athlete must operate according to the rules of his or her sport. Our culture has provided many examples of star athletes who have been banned or suspended from competition due to breaking rules related to performance-enhancing drugs or other violations. When an athlete cheats, that athlete is excluded from the possibility of winning.

This warning sounds like Paul's words in 1 Corinthians 3:12-13, "Now if anyone builds on this foundation with gold, silver, precious stones, wood, hay, straw, each one's work will become clear; for the Day will declare it, because it will be revealed by fire; and the fire will test each one's work, of what sort it is." Those who shortcut God's way for quick success in this life may fool other people, but no one will fool the Lord. At the judgment seat of Christ, only those who compete as an athlete who follows the rules will receive rewards.

A Hardworking Farmer

Paul's final example is the hardworking farmer. American culture has frequently highlighted the legendary work ethic of the farmer, something also often reflected in other cultures. Farmers must endure the often unenjoyable work of preparing the soil, planting seed, removing weeds, and harvesting a crop before its food can be appreciated. Yet there is also something special about being the first to pick a ripened fruit or vegetable, eating the freshest of produce available.

In our service to the Lord, we must endure like the hardworking farmer. We will face much difficulty in this life, but when we endure faithfully, we will enjoy the sweet fruit of our labors in the presence of the Lord, including the rewards we receive at the bema seat of Christ. How do we respond to the coming judgment seat we will one day face as believers? The late Adrian Rogers offers these inspiring words to bring focus to the application of this critical topic:

> You are unique. You are wonderful. When God brings you
> to the Judgment Seat of Christ, He's going to ask, "Are you

using what you have?" He will be looking at your heart, not comparing you to someone else. God is going to test your work of what *sort* it is, not how big it is. God is going to look at your attitude, not only what you did, but why you did it. God is going to look at your authority. Were you obeying Him and doing what He told you to do? "To obey is better than to sacrifice." God is going to look at your ability. Did you serve Him according to what He gave you?[19]

The biblical teaching on our heavenly rewards balances the grace of God with the believer's personal responsibility. It motivates us to live for Christ both in this life and the life to come. God leaves us here to make a difference in this world and in the world to come. In light of the Savior's promise: "Behold, I am coming quickly, and My reward is with Me, to give to every one according to his work" (Revelation 22:12), let us run the race to win the prize (Philippians 3:14).

As I mentioned earlier, I didn't have the privilege of growing up in a Christian home. I was led to Christ by Mrs. Johnson when I was a young boy attending Vacation Bible School. She had no clue at that time that this kid would grow up to teach over 100,000 students, speak to millions on television, and preach the gospel all over the world for the past fifty years. Mrs. Johnson will have incredible rewards in heaven as my "partner" in ministry. She will be rewarded for her faithful service to the Lord (see Matthew 10:40-42). Without ever leaving home, she has touched the world for Christ—not only through me but countless others as well.

The same can be true of you. Everything you do as a believer to serve the Lord will be rewarded. God is keeping the record book and will bless you for all that you have done for the cause of Christ and the gospel. One day, you will stand before the Lord at the bema seat judgment to receive your rewards. Oh, what a day that will be!

5

THE MARRIAGE OF THE LAMB: HERE COMES THE BRIDE

I have never really liked the movie *Father of the Bride*. It is hilariously funny, but sadly all too often true! The father of the bride gets stuck with all the heartaches, all the challenges, and all the bills. In the end, he is totally exhausted. Fortunately, our future wedding will not be like that. Our heavenly Father will orchestrate the entire ceremony gloriously.

If you are married, do you remember the day of your wedding? Wedding days are usually considered one of the most important days most of us will experience in this life. Ours certainly was. Many couples spend thousands of dollars and months (or even years) preparing for this event. In 2020, the average cost for an American wedding was nearly $34,000. The average engagement length is twelve to eighteen months. This is much more money and much longer time than we spend on nearly any other area of life. Unfortunately, some couples spend more time, energy, and money on their wedding than on their marriage. As a result, many marriages do not last.

In biblical times, weddings were important because marriage was important. Marriages involved covenant arrangements between two families. The father of the bride had to agree to give his daughter in marriage and the father of the groom had to bless the marriage, make the arrangements, and authorize the groom to get the bride when the preparations were completed.

Jewish weddings included much more fanfare in first-century Jewish culture. A wedding could last an entire week, included large family gatherings, and impacted the entire community. In John 2, we see a picture of this when Jesus performed His first miracle at a wedding. His very presence at the wedding in Cana at the beginning of His ministry forecast the wedding in heaven that will come when the bride of Christ is taken up into the Father's house. Jesus predicted this wedding through His parables (Matthew 22:1-14; 25:1-13; Luke 12:35-36).

Harold Wilmington states:

> The host of this marriage will be God the Father. He is pictured as preparing it and sending His servants out to invite the selected guests (Luke 14:16-23). The bridegroom is Jesus Christ, the Father's beloved Son (Matthew 3:17; 17:5)...The apostle Paul wrote concerning the church, "For I have betrothed you to one husband, that I may present you as a chaste virgin to Christ" (2 Corinthians 11:2).[1]

The six water jars Jesus filled at the wedding in Cana included enough wine for approximately 2,400 servings![2] Since this took place *after* the regular wine had already run out, there were likely several hundred or more people involved in this single wedding. Wine is one of the signs of messianic blessing (Isaiah 25:6). Rabbi Jason Sobel observes: "By turning water into wine, Jesus demonstrated that He was the promised prophet, the greater Moses who came that we might begin to experience the abundant life of the messianic kingdom here and now through faith in Messiah Jesus."[3]

Building on the parallels of the Jewish wedding tradition, the Bible speaks of a yet-future wedding called the marriage of the Lamb. This event will take place suddenly and dramatically. The same apostle John who wrote about Jesus performing His first miracle at a wedding in Cana details another, far more glorious wedding event in the book of

Revelation (19:6-9). It is as though we have finally arrived at what we have been waiting for all along. The church is the betrothed bride of Christ now during the present age, but our marriage to Him will be in the future.

The marriage of the Lamb has not yet taken place. The apostle Paul wrote, "For I have betrothed you to one husband, that I may present you as a chaste virgin to Christ" (2 Corinthians 11:2). He also adds that Christ "loved the church and gave Himself for her…that He might present her to Himself a glorious church, not having spot or wrinkle or any such thing, but that she should be holy and without blemish" (Ephesians 5:25-27).

The New Testament pictures the church as betrothed to Christ at this present time. A betrothal was similar to a wedding engagement in our time, yet much stronger. For example, Joseph was betrothed to Mary when he discovered she was pregnant by the Holy Spirit with Jesus. He originally planned to divorce her quietly, because a betrothal required an official separation similar to a divorce (Matthew 1:18-21). Therefore, our relationship to Christ is like a spiritual betrothal.

It is in this same manner that the apostle Paul refers to the sealing of the Holy Spirit as the "guarantee" (KJV, "earnest") of our salvation. The believer's baptism by the Spirit is the "engagement ring" or "guarantee" that Christ will fulfill His promises to us. Daniel Mitchell writes:

> This sealing has a threefold significance in the New Testament: 1. To indicate ownership 2. To indicate genuineness 3. To preserve and keep safe…Paul uses the term *arrabon* only three times and always in reference to the Holy Spirit as a down payment…The indwelling Spirit is the surety and the "security" of all that is to follow in the final salvation of the believer (cf. Rom. 8:9-11, 23; Eph 1:14; 2 Cor. 5:5).[4]

Today, believers in Christ make up the church that is betrothed to Him. We are still awaiting the "judgment seat of Christ" (2 Corinthians 5:10), presumably after the rapture and before the marriage, both of which take place in heaven. While Revelation 19 pictures

Christ symbolically as the Lamb (verse 7), the picture of the marriage is clearly expressed. The aorist tense of "has come" (Greek, *elthen*) indicates a completed act, showing that the wedding is now consummated.[5] Instead of the normal seven-day Jewish wedding ceremony, this one appears to last seven years (during the tribulation period). The marriage will be completed in heaven (Revelation 19:7), but the marriage supper will probably take place later on earth, where Israel is awaiting the return of Christ and the church.

This is the only way to distinguish the bridegroom (Christ), the bride (church), and the ten virgins (Israel) in Matthew 25:1-13. There is no way Jesus is coming to marry all ten (or five) of these women. They are the attendants (Old Testament saints and tribulation saints) at the wedding. Only the church is the bride. That is why Jesus could say of John the Baptist that there was not a "greater prophet" (Old Testament saint), but he that is "least in the kingdom of God" (the church) is "greater than he" (Luke 7:28). Like Old Testament saints, John the Baptist lived and died before the beginning of the church age (prior to Pentecost).

In this chapter, we'll discuss the aspect of the marriage supper of the Lamb as part of the amazing future we have to anticipate as followers of Christ. We'll look at the place, the participants, and the process involved in this glorious future marriage.

The Location: The Wedding Place

Where will this marriage of the Lamb take place? The marriage ceremony itself will follow in heaven during the tribulation period on earth. It must take place after the rapture yet before Christ returns to the earth at the end of the tribulation. Following the bema seat of Christ, Jesus will be united with His bride, the church. While aspects of this wedding will continue into the time of Christ's return and the millennial kingdom, the marriage itself will take place when the church goes to the Father's house to be with Christ.

This timing also fits well with the way families in the ancient Near East often expanded and lived together. A grown son would often be betrothed to a woman, yet the wedding did not take place until the son had prepared a home for them. This home was often an extension built onto the house or on the land that was owned by the son's father. When the new home or extension to the home was prepared, the couple would be married. The father would inspect the addition, approve it, and authorize the son to go get the bride. The husband and wife would then begin life together at the father's house in their new home or room, an analogy very similar to what Jesus shared in John 14:1-3.

There also remains some debate regarding the timing of the events related to this future marriage of the Lamb. For example, some suggest a difference between a marriage supper in heaven and a later marriage feast on earth. Others, myself included, view the marriage as taking place in heaven and the marriage supper taking place when Christ returns, extending into the millennial kingdom when both Jews and Gentiles will be invited and celebrate with the Lord.[6] Ron Rhodes notes more specifically that the marriage supper of the Lamb will unfold during the seventy-five-day interval between the end of the tribulation and the start of the millennial kingdom.[7]

Rhodes also references the research of Arnold Fruchtenbaum, who suggests the marriage ceremony will take place after the judgment seat of Christ:

> The marriage ceremony takes place in heaven and involves the church. That it must take place after the judgment seat of Messiah is evident from [Revelation 19:8], for the bride is viewed as being dressed in white linen, which is the righteous acts of the saints. This means that all the wood, hay, and stubble has been burned away and all the gold, silver, and precious stones have been purified. Thus, following the rapture of the church in which the Bridegroom brings the bride with Him to His home, and following the judgment seat of Messiah which results in the bride having the white linen garments, the wedding ceremony takes place.[8]

Tim LaHaye offers additional support regarding this timing of the marriage of the Lamb. He refers to Ephesians 5:27, "that He might present her to Himself a glorious church, not having spot or wrinkle or any such thing, but that she should be holy and without blemish." When will the church be without blemish? He notes:

> This condition will only exist after the judgment of Christ when believers have been completely cleansed and the Church is made whole. For that reason we believe that the Judgment Seat of Christ, which will take place during the Tribulation, will precede the marriage supper of the Lamb, and immediately after the judgment of reward has been presented to the last believer, the marriage of the Lamb will take place. All Christians who have trusted in Christ during the age of grace, from the day of Pentecost to the Rapture of the Church, will make up His Bride.[9]

John Walvoord adds, "As the marriage feast is the final stage, it should be clear that the Lamb has already come for His bride and claimed her previously in the rapture of the church."[10]

The Cast: The Wedding Participants

In modern weddings, a large cast may often be involved. In addition to the groom and bride, there is traditionally a minister, the parents of the bride and groom, a ring bearer, best man, maid of honor, bridesmaids, groomsmen, musicians, technical workers running sound and lights, and much more. Similarly, the marriage of the Lamb will include a cast of individuals who will participate in a wedding ceremony without comparison.

Mark Hitchcock identifies four key participants who will share in this marriage event. They will include the host (God the Father), the bridegroom (Jesus), the bride (the church), and the guests (Old Testament and tribulation saints).[11] Let's take a brief look at the role of each of these participants.

The Wedding Host (God the Father)

God the Father will serve as the host of this heavenly wedding. In Matthew 22:2-3, Jesus used the parable of the wedding feast to identify the Father's role: "The kingdom of heaven is like a certain king who arranged a marriage for his son, and sent out his servants to call those who were invited to the wedding; and they were not willing to come." Interestingly, Jesus notes the tradition of arranged marriage. The son did not choose his wife in the parable, a pattern common in the first century, particularly among kings who carefully selected who they considered the best spouse for their sons. This detail highlights the divine preparation God has made for our eternal communion with the Lord. We have been carefully chosen by the Father (2 Corinthians 11:2).

As believers, we have even been given a dowry by our Father—the indwelling Holy Spirit. Ephesians 1:13-14 says, "In Him you also trusted, after you heard the word of truth, the gospel of your salvation; in whom also, having believed, you were sealed with the Holy Spirit of promise, who is the guarantee of our inheritance until the redemption of the purchased possession, to the praise of His glory."

Our wedding host, God the Father, has selected us and gifted us with everything we need to serve in our role as part of the church in this future wedding celebration. As we noted in Ephesians 2:10 earlier, "For we are His workmanship, created in Christ Jesus for good works, which God prepared beforehand that we should walk in them." Our Father has prepared us, calling us to live in purity as we await our future marriage with the Lord.

The Bridegroom (Jesus)

In Luke 5:34-35, Jesus identified Himself as the bridegroom: "Can you make the friends of the bridegroom fast while the bridegroom is with them? But the days will come when the bridegroom will be taken away from them; then they will fast in those days" (also Mark 2:19-20). When Jesus died on the cross, His followers likely did fast and go without food as part of their mourning. The emphasis, however, rests on Jesus as the bridegroom. The Father serves as the host, while the Son serves as the groom.

John the Baptist also used this analogy when asked whether he was the Messiah. He answered, "The friend of the bridegroom, who stands and hears him, rejoices greatly because of the bridegroom's voice. Therefore this joy of mine is fulfilled" (John 3:29). John the Baptist recognized the relationship of Jesus as both Messiah and as the groom who would one day come to unite in marriage with His bride, the church.

The Bride (the Church)

Some have sought to connect this bride with Israel from the Old Testament. While this representation is made between Israel and the Lord, there are notable differences. Walvoord explains:

> In the Old Testament, Israel is represented as the wife of Jehovah untrue to her marriage vows but destined to be restored in the future kingdom. In the New Testament, the church is presented as the bride of Christ not yet claimed by the bridegroom but waiting as a virgin for the coming marriage union.[12]

Instead, the New Testament refers to the church as the bride of Christ. Paul writes in Ephesians 5:25-27:

> Husbands, love your wives, just as Christ also loved the church and gave Himself for her, that He might sanctify and cleanse her with the washing of water by the word, that He might present her to Himself a glorious church, not having spot or wrinkle or any such thing, but that she should be holy and without blemish.

The bride of Christ is clearly the church of the New Testament. We likewise see references to the church as the bride in 2 Corinthians 11:2 as well as in Matthew 25:1-13. Ray Stedman writes:

> It is a great honor to be invited to a wedding feast. It is a feast to which the entire human race is invited—but only a fraction of the human race will attend. The invitation is the gospel, and the gospel has gone out to all men and women everywhere, in every age of history. Some accept the invitation. Some reject it…The Spirit of God has been calling

men and women throughout the centuries, from Old Testament times through our own New Testament era and on into the future, even in the tribulation period. The invitation goes out to everyone: "Come to the marriage feast of the Lamb!" What a privilege that will be, to see the Bridegroom face to face, to be a member of His beloved bride, to share in the intimacy of fellowship with the Lord Jesus![13]

The Guests (Old Testament and Tribulation Saints)

Though the marriage of the Lamb will take place in heaven, the marriage feast or marriage supper will include events after the wedding ceremony that will take place on earth. Revelation 19:9 teaches, "Blessed are those who are called to the marriage supper of the Lamb!" These guests will include Old Testament believers and tribulation saints who will be resurrected at the second coming of Jesus to celebrate with Him in the millennial kingdom. Matthew 22:1-14 further supports this view, revealing a future time when those beyond the initial wedding gathering will join in the celebration with the wedding couple. Dwight Pentecost adds:

> The resurrection of Israel and the Old Testament saints will not take place until the second advent of Christ. Revelation 20:4-6 makes it equally clear that tribulation saints will not be resurrected until that time also. While it would be impossible to eliminate these groups from the place of observers, they cannot be in the position of participants in the event itself.[14]

The Plan: The Wedding Process

The analogy of the marriage of the Lamb with Jewish wedding customs offers a fascinating look at our amazing future as believers. Some divide the process into three parts (contract, ceremony, consummation). However, seven distinct aspects can be noted about the Jewish wedding process that include parallels with prophetic events.

Regarding the overall process of the Jewish wedding, Tony Garland explains:

> First, the father of the groom made the arrangements
> for the marriage and paid the bride price. The timing of
> the arrangement varied. Sometimes it occurred when
> both children were small, and at other times it was a year
> before the marriage itself. Often the bride and groom
> did not even meet until their wedding day. The second
> step, which occurred a year or more after the first step,
> was the fetching of the bride. The bridegroom would
> go to the home of the bride in order to bring her to
> his home. [15]

These two aspects further divide into the seven areas of 1) covenant (the betrothal), 2) the chamber (the bride's home), 3) the coming (the rapture), 4) the cleansing (the bride's preparation), 5) the ceremony (the wedding), 6) the consummation (the union), and 7) the celebration (marriage feast). Let's look at each of these areas in relation to the marriage of the Lamb.

Part 1: The Covenant (the Betrothal)

The beginning of the marriage includes preparation. In ancient Jewish wedding customs, like many other ancient Near Eastern cultures, marriages were generally arranged. Hitchcock notes, "The betrothal agreement was solemnized by three acts: (1) a solemn oral commitment in the presence of witnesses, (2) a pledge of money, and (3) a written pledge or contract."[16] One article notes:

> The *Shulkhan Arukh*, an exhaustive presentation of the
> details of Jewish law, elaborates regarding the two stages of
> marriage: the betrothal (*kiddushin*, meaning "sanctified")
> and the consummation of the marriage (*nisuin*, translated
> "elevation"). *Kiddushin* is not engagement as we understand
> it. It is a binding agreement in which the woman is legally
> considered the wife of the man. It was routine in Jesus' day

for *kiddushin* and *nisuin* to be separated by as much as a year.[17]

Several biblical passages also reveal the Lord's purchase of the church as part of our marriage preparations. For example, Paul exhorts the elders in the church at Ephesus in Acts 20:28, "Therefore take heed to yourselves and to all the flock, among which the Holy Spirit has made you overseers, to shepherd the church of God which He purchased with His own blood." Jesus purchased believers with the most valuable resource possible—His own life.

First Corinthians 6:20 adds, "For you were bought at a price; therefore glorify God in your body and in your spirit, which are God's." Our salvation is a free gift, but its cost was great, involving the agonizing death of our Lord upon the cross. Robert Mounce also explains the betrothal as one of the two major events involved in marriage in biblical times:

> In Biblical times a marriage involved two major events, the betrothal and the wedding. These were normally separated by a period of time during which the two individuals were considered husband and wife and as such were under the obligations of faithfulness. The wedding began with a procession to the bride's house, which was followed by a return to the house of the groom for the marriage feast. By analogy, the church, espoused to Christ by faith, now awaits the *parousia* when the heavenly groom will come for his bride and return to heaven for the marriage feast which lasts throughout eternity.[18]

Part 2: The Chamber (the Bride's Home)

Following the betrothal agreement, there was generally an extended time until the bridegroom would arrive for his wife. Hampton Keathley explains:

> During the betrothal phase the groom would prepare an apartment, a place to live in his father's house. Homes,

especially for the wealthy, were often very large complexes. Only the portions which were needed, however, were finished and furnished. When a son was to be married, another portion was completed to make ready for the new bride (John 14:2-3). The rapture, or resurrection and transformation of the church, is the event which brings the groom to the bride and which takes the bride back into heaven.[19]

As we noted in our discussion regarding the Father's house in John 14:1-3, Jesus speaks of going to prepare a place for us where there are many rooms. Though the King James Version uses the word "mansions," which has given rise to the thought of each believer living in a palatial mansion, the more accurate understanding involves one large house with adequate space for the bride of Christ to dwell.

In this biblical imagery, Christ has purchased the church with His own blood. He now dwells in heaven with the Father and is preparing our future home with Him (John 6:62; Acts 1:9-11). Think about it: Jesus has been working on our heavenly dwelling for nearly two thousand years. Our future home will surpass anything we can imagine! It will offer a perfect home with our Lord where we will live from the time of His coming at the rapture until the time we return with Him at the second coming to reign with Him in His millennial kingdom.

Part 3: The Coming (the Rapture)

The third aspect of the wedding process between Jesus and the bride of Christ includes the rapture. The betrothal took place at the cross. Jesus is now preparing our future home. The rapture is the next step we await, an event that will take place at any moment. In relation with Jewish wedding customs, Garland explains:

> In connection with this step, two other things should be noted. *First*, it was the father of the groom who determined the timing. *Second*, prior to the groom's leaving to fetch the bride, he must already have a place prepared

for her as their abode. This was followed by the third step, the wedding ceremony, to which a few would be invited. Prior to the wedding ceremony, the bride underwent a ritual immersion for ritual cleansing. The fourth step, the marriage feast, would follow and could last for as many as seven days. Many more people would be invited to the feast than were to the marriage ceremony. In the Marriage of the Lamb all four of these steps of the Jewish wedding ceremony are evident.[20]

Though we have already discussed the rapture, the three primary biblical passages related to the rapture are:

John 14:1-3: "Let not your heart be troubled; you believe in God, believe also in Me. In My Father's house are many mansions; if it were not so, I would have told you. I go to prepare a place for you. And if I go and prepare a place for you, I will come again and receive you to Myself; that where I am, there you may be also."

1 Corinthians 15:51-52: Behold, I tell you a mystery: We shall not all sleep, but we shall all be changed—in a moment, in the twinkling of an eye, at the last trumpet. For the trumpet will sound, and the dead will be raised incorruptible, and we shall be changed.

1 Thessalonians 4:15-18: For this we say to you by the word of the Lord, that we who are alive and remain until the coming of the Lord will by no means precede those who are asleep. For the Lord Himself will descend from heaven with a shout, with the voice of an archangel, and with the trumpet of God. And the dead in Christ will rise first. Then we who are alive and remain shall be caught up together with them in the clouds to meet the Lord in the air. And thus we shall always be with the Lord. Therefore comfort one another with these words.

The principles found in these passages reflect many aspects of Jewish wedding traditions. Thomas Constable explains:

> [W]hen the time for marriage (the wedding ceremony) had come, the groom would leave his home with his friends, go to the home of the bride, and escort her from her home to his. The bride did not know when this would occur, just as Christians do not know when the Rapture will occur. This will take place when Christ comes to take His bride from her home, earth, to His home, heaven—at the Rapture—for their wedding (cf. John 14:1-2).[21]

As the bride of Christ, our role is to eagerly await the coming of our future husband, the Lord Jesus Christ, at the any-moment rapture of the church.

Part 4: The Cleansing (the Bride's Preparation)

Another aspect of the Jewish wedding ceremony is the bride's preparation and separation from the time of trial that will take place upon the earth during the seven-year tribulation. Believers will experience rewards as God provides (1 Corinthians 3:12-15) and remain in the Father's house from the time of the rapture until the second coming at the end of the tribulation period. Renald Showers notes:

> Corresponding with the Jewish bride remaining hidden in the bridal chamber for a period of seven days after arrival at the groom's father's house, the Church will remain hidden for a period of seven [years] after arrival at Christ's Father's house in heaven. While the seven-year Tribulation Period is taking place on the earth, the Church will be in heaven totally hidden from the sight of those living on the earth. Just as the Jewish groom brought his bride out of the bridal chamber at the conclusion of the seven days with her veil removed, so that all could see who his bride was, so Christ will bring His Church out of heaven in His Second Coming at the conclusion of the seven-year Tribulation Period

in full view of all who are alive, so that all can see who the true church is (Col. 3:4).[22]

We see a hint of this in Revelation 19:7-8: "His wife has made herself ready. And to her it was granted to be arrayed in fine linen, clean and bright, for the fine linen is the righteous acts of the saints." While some see an application in these words for believers to prepare through pure living for this future time, this aspect involves a purity only Christ can provide. He gives us, His bride, fine clothing for the wedding. We do not have the ability to live spotless lives in our own power. While the directive to live a holy life is true, this particular part of our future with the Lord is based on His purifying work in our lives.

Part 5: The Ceremony (the Wedding)

Steve Herzig offers an insightful comparison of the Jewish wedding feast in relationship to the end times:

> On the Sabbath before the wedding, the groom is "called up" (*aliya*) to the *bema* (*platform*) to read the Torah. The congregation showers him with candies, representing wishes for a sweet married life. Other preparations include the bride purchasing a *tallit* (*prayer shawl*) for her husband-to-be and a period of fasting by the couple, signifying their sorrow for sin and their desire for a new beginning. The man and woman separately immerse themselves into the ritual bath called the *mikveh*, which is a bath of natural water instituted for the purpose of sanctification. As they immerse themselves, they proclaim their devotion to one another and separation from others.[23]

Interestingly, the marriage between Christ and the church will follow the bema seat judgment. Believers will be united with the Lord and committed into His care within the Father's house. Believers will be purified and spotless, no longer able to sin, while dwelling in perfect union with the Lord.

Part 6: The Consummation (the Union)

Revelation 19:7 describes the bride of Christ: "Let us be glad and rejoice and give Him glory, for the marriage of the Lamb has come, and His wife has made herself ready." As Showers further notes regarding the union of the Jewish groom and bride:

> Shortly after arrival the bride and groom would be escorted by the other members of the wedding party to the bridal chamber (*huppah*). Prior to entering the chamber the bride remained veiled so that no one could see her face. While the groomsmen and bridesmaids would wait outside, the bride and groom would enter the bridal chamber alone. There in the privacy of that place they would enter into physical union for the first time, thereby consummating the marriage that had been covenanted earlier.[24]

It appears the consummation of the marriage of the Lamb takes place prior to Christ's actual coming to the earth at Armageddon. Further, the purity of the bride of Christ is contrasted with the actions of the unrighteous harlot described in Revelation 17–18. Keathley observes:

> Following the parenthetical sections of chapters 17–18 which described the great harlot system of Babylon, chapter 19 gives us heaven's perspective of the fall of Babylon. Heaven's perspective stands in stark contrast to the mourning of Babylon's lovers, and it resumes the progress and narrative of the future events of the Tribulation. With chapters 17–18 as a background, John receives new revelation concerning the return of the Lord Jesus Christ.[25]

Part 7: The Celebration (the Marriage Feast)

The marriage feast of the Lamb will extend beyond the marriage union of the Lord Jesus Christ and His church in heaven. The feast will include Christ's coming to the earth with us, the bride of Christ, to celebrate. This feast will include both the destruction of Christ's enemies at Armageddon, as well as the gathering of the groom, bride, and their other guests in the feast that will extend into the millennial kingdom.[26]

It is during this time that the other guests will include both Old Testament believers as well as tribulation saints. This aspect is pictured in the parable of the wedding feast in Matthew 22:8-10:

> Then he said to his servants, "The wedding is ready, but those who were invited were not worthy. Therefore go into the highways, and as many as you find, invite to the wedding." So those servants went out into the highways and gathered together all whom they found, both bad and good. And the wedding hall was filled with guests.

Further, those who rejected the Messiah will then be destroyed and enter into eternal punishment. This rejection is noted in the rest of the parable of the wedding feast (vv. 11-14), as well as three times in Matthew 25 (vv. 11-12,30,46).

How to Live Prepared for the Marriage of the Lamb

As amazing as this future marriage between Christ and the church appears, is there any way in which this impacts our lives today? The answer is yes! Two important applications emerge from our study of this topic. First, we are called to live pure lives before the Lord. We do not want Him to return to find us wasting our lives and abusing His grace. The Great Commandment calls us to love the Lord our God with all our heart, soul, and mind, and to love our neighbor as ourselves (Matthew 22:34-40).

Second, Scripture clearly indicates we are to help everyone possible come to faith in Christ. The Great Commission teaches we are to make disciples of all nations (Matthew 28:18-20). Our focus must not be only on ourselves, but also upon helping others know the Lord and to prepare for His coming. Positively, we desire for every person possible to enjoy this marriage in heaven with the Lord. Negatively, we also want to help others escape the tragic judgments that await during the tribulation period, as well as the prospect of eternal separation from

God. The marriage supper of the Lamb serves as both a glorious future to anticipate as well as a motivating factor for devotion to Christ today.

Every believer has a marriage in their future. No matter whether you have never been married nor how many times you may have been married, you have a marriage coming when Jesus returns for His bride. He is definitely coming again. The question is: Is He coming for you?

6

THE TRIUMPHANT RETURN: WHEN JESUS COMES AS KING

The second coming of Christ is the most anticipated event in human history. It is the ultimate fulfillment of our Lord's promise to return. It is also the culmination of all biblical prophecy. The return of Christ is the final apologetic! Once He returns, there will be no further need to debate His claims or the validity of the Christian message. The King will come in person to set the record straight.[1]

Revelation 19 is probably the most dramatic chapter in the entire Bible. It is the final capstone to the death and resurrection of Christ. In this chapter the living Savior returns to earth to crush all satanic opposition to the truth. He establishes His kingdom on earth in fulfillment of the Old Testament prophecies of His own promise to return.

Just before the crucifixion, the disciples asked Jesus, "What will be the sign of Your coming?" (Matthew 24:3). Our Lord replied, "Immediately after the tribulation of those days…the powers of the heavens will be shaken. Then the sign of the Son of Man will appear in heaven, and then all the tribes of the earth will mourn, and they will see the Son of Man coming on the clouds of heaven with power and great glory" (vv. 29-30).

As Jesus looked down the corridor of time to the end of the present age, He warned of a time of great tribulation that would come upon the whole world (vv. 4-28). Our Lord went on to explain that the devastation of the great tribulation will be so extensive that unless those days were cut short, "no one would survive" (v. 22 NIV). Jesus further described this coming day of trouble as a time when the sun and moon will be darkened and the heavens will be shaken (v. 29). His description runs parallel to that found in Revelation 16:1-16, where the final hour of the tribulation is depicted by atmospheric darkness and ecological disaster.

The return of Christ is a twofold event. It marks both the final defeat of the Antichrist and the final triumph of Christ. René Pache writes, "The main event announced by the prophets is not the judgment of the world, nor the restoration of Israel, nor even the triumph of the Church: it is the glorious advent of the Son of God."[2] Without Him, there is no hope of a better future. He is the central figure of the world to come. It is His kingdom and we are His bride. Oh, what a day that will be!

David Jeremiah observes:

> Although Christians are most familiar with the first coming of Christ, it is the second coming that gets the most ink in the Bible. References to the second coming outnumber references to the first by a factor of eight to one. Scholars count 1,845 biblical references to the second coming, including 318 in the New Testament. Christ's return is emphasized in no less than seventeen Old Testament books and seven out of every ten chapters in the New Testament. The Lord Himself referred to His return twenty-one times. The second coming is second only to faith as the most dominant subject in the New Testament.[3]

The Promise of His Return

Jesus promised His disciples in the upper room that He was going to heaven to prepare a place for them. Then He said, "And if I go and prepare a place for you, I will come again, and receive you to Myself: that where I am, there you may be also" (John 14:3). Even though the early disciples eventually died, the Bible promised, "Behold, I tell you a mystery: We shall not all sleep [die], but we shall all be changed [resurrected or raptured]—in a moment, in the twinkling of an eye, at the last trumpet. For the trumpet will sound, and the dead will be raised incorruptible, and we shall be changed" (1 Corinthians 15:51-52).

The apostle Paul reiterates this same hope in 1 Thessalonians 4:14,16-17, when he comments about those believers who have already died and gone to heaven. He says, "For if we believe that Jesus died and rose again, even so God will bring with Him [from heaven] those who have fallen asleep [died] in Jesus…For the Lord Himself will descend from heaven with a shout, with the voice of the archangel and with the trumpet of God; and the dead in Christ will rise first. Then we who are alive and remain will be caught up together with them in the clouds to meet the Lord in the air" (NASB).

The promise to return for the church (believers of the church age) is the promise of the rapture. When Revelation 19 opens, the church is already in heaven with Christ at the marriage supper. The rapture has already occurred. Jesus is depicted as the groom and the church as the bride. The marriage supper celebrates their union after the rapture and before their return to earth.

One of the greatest interpretive problems for nonrapturists is to explain how the church got to heaven *prior* to the second coming. Surely they were not all martyred, or else Paul's comments about "we who are alive and remain" (1 Thessalonians 4:15,17) would be meaningless. The rapture must be presumed to have occurred before the events in Revelation 19—amillennialists and postmillennialists notwithstanding.[4]

The position of the church (bride of the Lamb) in Revelation 19:6-10 in *heaven* is crucial to the interpretation of the entire Apocalypse. New Testament scholar Robert Gromacki points out, "The Church is not mentioned during the seal, trumpet and bowl judgments because the Church is not here during the outpouring of these judgments."[5] He points out that the term for *church* (Greek, *ekklesia*) appears frequently in chapters 1–3 of Revelation. In fact, it is used nineteen times in those chapters. But the word *church* does not appear again until 22:16. In the meantime, the church is referred to in 19:7-10 as the bride of the Lamb.

The concept of the church as the bride or wife of Christ is clearly stated in Ephesians 5:22-23, where husbands are admonished to love their wives as Christ loved the church and gave Himself for her that He might present her in heaven as a glorious bride. There can be no doubt, therefore, that John intends for us to see the Lamb's "wife" as the church—the bride of Christ.

The Nature of Christ's Return

Jesus promised not only to return for His church, but He also promised to return to judge the world and to establish His kingdom on earth. His brother James refers to believers as "heirs of the kingdom which He promised to those who love Him" (James 2:5). Jesus Himself told His disciples that He would not drink the fruit of the vine after the Last Supper until He drank it with them in His Father's kingdom (Matthew 26:29). After the resurrection, they asked Him, "Lord, will You at this time restore the kingdom to Israel?" (Acts 1:6). He replied that the time was in the Father's hands. All these references imply a future kingdom when Christ returns.

The details of Christ's return include the following:

1. ***He will return personally.*** Paul said, "For the Lord Himself will descend from heaven with a shout" (1 Thessalonians 4:16). Jesus promised He would return in person (Matthew 24:30).

2. ***He will appear as the Son of Man.*** Since Pentecost, Christ has ministered through the Holy Spirit (John 14:16-23; 16:5-15). But when He returns, He will appear as the Son of Man in His glorified human form (Matthew 24:30; 26:64; Daniel 7:13-14).

3. ***He will return literally and visibly.*** In Acts 1:11, the angels promised, "This Jesus, who has been taken up from you

into heaven, will come in just the same way as you have watched Him go into heaven" (NASB). Revelation 1:7 tells us, "Every eye will see him, even those who pierced him; and all the tribes of the earth will mourn over Him" (NASB).

4. **He will come suddenly and dramatically.** Paul warned, "The day of the Lord will come just like a thief in the night" (1 Thessalonians 5:2). Jesus said, "For as the lightning comes from the east and flashes to the west, so also will the coming of the Son of Man be" (Matthew 24:27).

5. **He will come on the clouds of heaven.** Jesus said, "They will see the Son of Man coming on the clouds of heaven" (Matthew 24:30 [see Daniel 7:13; Luke 21:27]). Revelation 1:7 says, "Behold, He is coming with clouds."

6. **He will come in a display of glory.** Matthew 16:27 promises, "The Son of man will come in the glory of His Father." Matthew 24:30 adds, "They will see the Son of Man coming...with power and great glory."

7. **He will come with all His angels.** Jesus promised, "And He will send His angels with a great sound of a trumpet" (Matthew 24:31). Jesus said in one of His parables "The reapers are the angels...so it will be at the end of this age" (Matthew 13:39-40).

8. **He will come with His bride**—the church. That, of course, is the whole point of Revelation 19. Colossians 3:3 adds, "When Christ...appears, then you also will appear with Him in glory." Zechariah 14:5 adds, "Then the LORD, my God, will come, and all the holy ones with Him!" (NASB).

9. **He will return to the Mount of Olives.** "And in that day His feet will stand on the Mount of Olives" (Zechariah 14:4). Where the glory of God ascended into heaven, it will return (cf. Ezekiel 11:23). Where Jesus ascended into heaven, He will return (cf. Acts 1:3-12).

10. **He will return in triumph and victory.** Zechariah 14:9

promises, "And the LORD will be king over all the earth."
Revelation 19:16 depicts him as "KING OF KINGS AND
LORD OF LORDS." He will triumph over the Antichrist,
the false prophet, and Satan himself (Revelation 19:19-21).

Hallelujah, What a Savior!

Revelation 19 opens with a heavenly chorus, a "great multitude"
singing the praises of God (v. 1). Beasley-Murray calls it a "*Te Deum*
[hymn of praise to God] on the righteous judgments of God."[6] The
heavenly choir rejoices with praise because justice has finally been
served: "True and righteous are His judgments," they sing, "because
He has judged the great harlot" (v. 2). The praise chorus then breaks
into a fourfold alleluia in verses 1-6:

1. "Alleluia! Salvation and glory and honor and power belong
   to the Lord our God!" (v. 1).

2. "Alleluia! Her smoke rises up forever and ever!" (v. 3).

3. They "worshiped God who sat on the throne saying,
   'Amen! Alleluia!'" (v. 4).

4. "Alleluia! For the Lord God Omnipotent reigns!" (v. 6).

This is the only place in the New Testament where *alleluia* (or *hal-
lelujah*) occurs. It is a Hebrew word ("Praise Yah [Jehovah]"). It was
transliterated from the Hebrew into Greek and passed on into English. The same thing occurred with *amen, hosanna,* and *maranatha.*
The use of the four alleluias emphasizes the magnitude of this praise
and worship.

Beasley-Murray observes that these alleluias are reminiscent of the
Hallel Psalms (113–118), which were sung at the Jewish Passover meal.[7]
The first two (113–114) were sung before the meal and the last four
after the meal. Just as Israel sang God's praises for His deliverance in
the Passover, so the church in heaven sings God's praise for His deliverance from the Antichrist. The triumphal praise is very similar to that
heard earlier in Revelation 11:15-19. But the triumph that is heralded

is more than that over the downfall of "Babylon." It is the marriage of the Lamb that takes center stage in this cantata of praise.

Marriage of the Lamb

The sense of movement that is always prevalent in the Apocalypse now reaches a climax. "The marriage of the Lamb has come" (Revelation 19:7). It is as though we have finally arrived at what we have been waiting for all along. The wedding is finally here. It is obvious that John the revelator views this as a future (not past) event. The final culmination of the spiritual union between the Lamb and His bride has finally arrived.

Beasley-Murray expresses it like this: "The perfection in glory of the *Bride* belongs to the eschatological future! Therefore, the *now* and the *not yet* of the New Testament doctrine of salvation in the kingdom of God is perfectly exemplified. The Church is the Bride of Christ now, but her marriage lies in the future."[8]

This is exactly why we cannot say that the consummation of the marriage has already taken place. The apostle Paul says, "For I have betrothed you to one husband, that I may present you as a chaste virgin to Christ" (2 Corinthians 11:2). He also adds that Christ "loved the church and gave Himself for her...that He might present her to Himself a glorious church, not having spot or wrinkle or any such thing, but that she should be holy and without blemish" (Ephesians 5:25-27).

Bruce Metzger comments, "The concept of the relationship between God and his people as a marriage goes back into the Old Testament. Again and again the prophets spoke of Israel as the chosen Bride of God (Is. 54:1-8; Ezek. 16:7,8; Hos. 2:19). In the New Testament the Church is represented as the Bride of Christ...In the words of a familiar hymn: 'With his own blood he bought her, and for her life he died.'"[9]

The Triumphal Return

The singular vignette of Christ's return in Revelation 19:11-16 is the most dramatic passage in the entire Bible. In these six verses we are swept up into the triumphal entourage of redeemed saints as they ride in the heavenly procession with the King of kings and Lord of lords. In this one passage alone, all the hopes and dreams of every believer are finally and fully realized. This is not the Palm Sunday procession with the humble Messiah on the donkey colt. This is the ultimate in eschatological drama. The rejected Savior returns in triumph as the rightful King of all the world—*and we are with Him!*

Metzger notes, "From here on the tempo of the action increases. The ultimate outcome cannot be in doubt, but there are some surprises ahead, with the suspense of the drama sustained to the conclusion. From verse 11 to the first verse of chapter 21, we have in rapid succession seven visions preparatory to the end. Each of these begins with the word, 'I saw.'"[10]

The description of the triumphant Savior is that of a king leading an army to victory. The passage itself is the final phase of the seventh bowl of judgment begun in 16:17-21, moving through the details of 17:1–18:24 and on to chapter 19. Robert Thomas observes: "The final song of 19:1-8 celebrates the marriage of the warrior-Messiah...This agrees closely with traditional Jewish eschatology. The O.T. prophets foresaw the Lord coming in the Last Days as a man of war to dash his enemies in pieces and establish a kingdom over the nations (e.g., Isaiah 13:4; 31:4; 42:13; Ezek. 38–39; Joel 3; Zech. 14:3)."[11]

As the scene unfolds, heaven opens to reveal the Christ and to release the army of the redeemed. The description of their being clothed in bright, clean linen (Revelation 19:14) emphasizes the garments of the bride already mentioned earlier (v. 8). In this vignette, the bride appears as the army of the Messiah. But unlike contemporary apocalyptic dramas of that time (e.g., War Scroll of the Qumran sect), the victory is won without any military help from the faithful. This army has no weapons, no swords, no shields, and no armor. They are merely clad in the righteousness of the saints. They have not come to fight but to watch. They have not come to assist but to celebrate. The Messiah-King will do the fighting. He will win the battle by the power of His spoken word.

The Twelvefold Description of the King

The twelvefold description of the coming King (Revelation 19:11-16) combines elements of symbolism from various biblical passages and from the other pictures of the risen Christ in the book of Revelation. Notice the details of His appearance:

1. His Conquest: He rides the white horse (Revelation 6:2).

Revelation 19 describes Jesus arriving on a white horse. This is similar to the white horse in Revelation 6:2 ridden by a conqueror. A white horse symbolized victory. Unlike the usurper who rides the white horse in chapter 6, this rider is called "Faithful and True" (v. 11). Jesus will return to win in battle over Satan and His enemies in fulfillment of numerous prophecies regarding His second coming.

2. His Character: He is called Faithful and True (Revelation 3:14).

The declaration of Jesus as the faithful and true one in Revelation 19 connects with the message to the church at Laodicea in Revelation 3:14: "These things says the Amen, the Faithful and True Witness, the Beginning of the creation of God." The context of Revelation 3 and the messages to the seven churches clearly indicate Jesus is speaking. It is the magnitude of His character that will ultimately triumph over evil.

3. His Commission: He judges and makes war (2 Thessalonians 1:7-8).

In 2 Thessalonians 1:7-8, Paul speaks about Jesus, saying He will "give you who are troubled rest with us when the Lord Jesus is revealed from heaven with His mighty angels, in flaming fire taking vengeance on those who do not know God, and on those who do not obey the gospel of our Lord Jesus Christ." Paul clearly and accurately describes the second coming. Jesus will return from heaven with His angels, judging unbelievers in war against those who oppose Him.

4. His Clarity: His eyes are like a flame of fire (Revelation 1:14).

Revelation 1:14 describes Jesus in His glorified state: "His head and hair were white like wool, as white as snow, and His eyes like a flame of fire." These words echo Revelation 19:12 where Jesus returns with similar eyes: "His eyes were like a flame of fire." This indicates the penetration of His omniscient gaze into the souls of men.

5. His Coronation: He wears many crowns (Revelation 4:10).

Likewise, Revelation 4:10 also describes the glorified Jesus as receiving many crowns: "The twenty-four elders fall down before Him who sits on the throne and worship Him who lives forever and ever, and cast their crowns before the throne." This closely connects with Revelation 19:12 where we read, "On His head were many crowns" (Greek, *diadems*). He returns wearing the multiple crowns of His Kingship.

6. His Code: His secret name (Judges 13:18; Isaiah 9:6).

Revelation 19:12 indicates that He is identified with the secret, unspoken name of God. The I AM of the Old Testament (YHVH) was held in such high regard that His name was unspoken (Exodus 3:13-15). The revelation of this name makes public the name of the Messiah. Isaiah spoke of the coming Jewish Messiah in 9:6, declaring: "And His name will be called Wonderful, Counselor, Mighty God, Everlasting Father, Price of Peace." The second coming of Jesus will reveal the child born in the manger is the one who rules the world, equal with God the Father.

7. His Clothing: Robe dipped in blood (Isaiah 63:1-6).

Revelation 19:13 includes the note, "He was clothed with a robe dipped in blood," referring to the blood of His enemies. These words closely reflect the prophecy of Isaiah 63:1-6. For example, verses 2-3 tell us:

> Why is Your apparel red,
> And Your garments like one who treads in the winepress?
> "I have trodden the winepress alone,
> And from the peoples no one was with Me.
> For I have trodden them in My anger,
> And trampled them in My fury;

> Their blood is sprinkled upon My garments,
> And I have stained all My robes."

These graphic insights show the second coming will include much violence. During Christ's first coming, He shed His own blood. At the second coming, He will shed the blood of His enemies, bringing judgment upon those who have opposed Him.

8. His Confirmation: Called the Word of God (John 1:1).

Revelation 19:13 identifies the being at the second coming as "The Word of God." This phrase closely connects with the apostle John's words to begin his Gospel, where we read, "In the beginning was the Word, and the Word was with God, and the Word was God." Further, the mention of Jesus as the "Word of God" also identifies Him as more than just the Messiah, but as equal with God the Father. Jesus was "in the beginning with God" (John 1:2) and is co-eternal and co-existent with the Father and the Holy Spirit. John 1:3 adds, "All things were made through Him, and without Him nothing was made that was made." The author of creation will return at the second coming to redeem His world and reign from His throne as Scripture declares.

9. His Communication: Sword is in His mouth (Revelation 19:15,21).

He who created the world by His spoken word will conquer the world by that word. Revelation 19:15 notes a sharp sword from the mouth of Jesus that will strike the nations. Similarly, in Revelation 2:16, Jesus says He "will fight against them with the sword of My mouth." This is clearly the Lord, the one spoken of as the Messiah in Isaiah 49:2:

> And He has made My mouth like a sharp sword;
> In the shadow of His hand He has hidden Me,
> And made Me a polished shaft;
> In His quiver He has hidden Me.

The Lord will use the sword of His mouth to conquer His enemies and establish His kingdom at this final battle. He speaks and the battle is over! The greatest conflagration in human history comes to an end with Christ and His church at last victorious.

10. His Command: Rules with a rod of iron (Psalm 2:9).

In Revelation 19:15, Christ states He will "rule them with a rod of iron." This is one of three times the phrase "rod of iron" is used in Revelation. In 2:27, Jesus predicts, "He shall rule them with a rod of iron." In 12:5, the male Child (Jesus) "was to rule all nations with a rod of iron." These prophecies connect with the words of the psalmist in Psalm 2:9:

> You shall break them with a rod of iron;
> You shall dash them to pieces like a potter's vessel.

This is clearly the Messiah, the one who says in 2:7,

> I will declare the decree:
> The LORD has said to Me,
> "You are My Son,
> Today I have begotten You."

Jesus will fulfill this promise when He returns, wielding ultimate authority in a new millennial kingdom where we will reign with Him.

11. His Conquest: Treads the winepress of the wrath of God (Revelation 14:14-20).

We've already mentioned the connection of the winepress with Isaiah 63. However, this fulfillment at the second coming also connects with John's earlier words in Revelation 14. The graphic description is given of God's judgment in verse 20: "And the winepress was trampled outside the city, and blood came out of the winepress, up to the horses' bridles, for one thousand six hundred furlongs."

The height of a horse's bridle is usually estimated at about four and a half feet. The distance of the bloody image in this prediction of 1,600 furlongs (or literally 1,600 stadia) is approximately 180 miles. This would indicate an area larger than only Armageddon, extending beyond to neighboring locations beyond the Jezreel Valley. Regardless of the exact details, the gruesome picture depicted here indicates the most destructive judgment possible, completely annihilating the enemies of God.

12. His Celebration: King of kings and Lord of lords (Revelation 17:14).

The name King of kings and Lord of lords found in Revelation 19:16 is used in Scripture to describe the greatest of leaders (Ezra 7:12; Ezekiel 26:7; Daniel 2:37,47). In the New Testament, it is used in 1 Timothy 6:15 about Jesus. Revelation 17:14 is the one other mention of this name in John's prophecy, where the name is also associated with the Lamb. Similarly, those with Him are described as "called, chosen, and faithful." As Warren Wiersbe notes:

> This description of Christ is thrilling! He is no longer on a humble donkey, but on a fiery white charger. His eyes are not filled with tears as when He beheld Jerusalem; nor is He wearing a mocking crown of thorns. Instead of being stripped by His enemies, He wears a garment dipped in blood, signifying judgment and victory. When on earth, He was abandoned by His followers; but here the armies of heaven follow Him in conquest. His mouth does not speak "words of grace" (Luke 4:22), but rather the Word of victory and justice.[12]

The Savior returns from heaven with His bride at His side. The church militant is now the church triumphant. Her days of conflict, rejection, and persecution are over. She returns victorious with her Warrior-King-Husband. The German pietist A.W. Boehm put it best when he wrote:

> There will be a time when the Church of Christ will come up from the wilderness of her crosses and afflictions, leaning upon her Beloved, and in his power bidding defiance to all her enemies. Then shall the Church...appear Terrible

as an Army with banners, but terrible to those only that despised her while she was in her minority and would not have her Beloved to reign over them.[13]

Every true believer who reads the prediction of Christ's triumph in Revelation 19:11-16 is overwhelmed by its significance. We are also overcome by its personal implications, for each of us will be in that heavenly army that returns with Him from glory. In fact, you might want to take a pen and circle the word *armies* in 19:14 and write your name in the margin of your Bible next to it, for *every believer* will be there when He returns.

The destiny of the true believer is now fully clarified. Our future hope includes rapture, return, and reign. No matter what one's eschatological viewpoint, the church must be raptured to heaven prior to the marriage supper and prior to her return from heaven with Christ. In the rapture, we go up to heaven. In the return, we come back to earth. In the millennium, we reign with Christ on the earth for a thousand years (Revelation 20:4-6).

How Will Jesus Return?

We've discussed the chronology of Jesus' return at His second coming, as well as the twelvefold description of the King. In addition, Scripture also reveals seven aspects of how Jesus will return that encourage us regarding our amazing future with Him.

Personally

Of utmost importance is the promise that Christ will return personally. He will not send others on His behalf but will be intimately involved with the culmination of His prophetic plans. In Acts 1:10-11, the disciples looked at the sky where Jesus had ascended to the Father in heaven. Two angels appeared, saying, "Men of Galilee, why do you stand gazing up into heaven? This same Jesus, who was taken up from you into heaven, will so come in like manner as you saw Him go into heaven." Just as Jesus personally left this world, He will personally return to it.

Revelation 22:20 also assures us of His personal involvement: "He who testifies to these things says, 'Surely I am coming quickly.'" Jesus does not say He will send for us; He will come for us. The one who made us and sustains us will return for us at the rapture and return with us at the second coming to establish a throne that will ultimately last for all eternity.

Literally

I am amazed at those who argue Jesus will fulfill His prophecies only symbolically. While some aspects of Bible prophecy are symbolic, His second coming will result in the literal fulfillment of multiple predictions. Revelation 19 offers numerous details of Jesus literally coming, unleashing judgment, and defeating His enemies. He will not outsource His victory but will appear in person for this final battle at the end of the tribulation period, and we will be with Him (Revelation 19:14). Jesus returns with His bride, not to spare the church, but to spare the human race. He Himself predicted, "Unless those days were shortened, no flesh would be saved" (Matthew 24:22).

Visibly

In many films about the rapture, those who go to be with the Lord simply disappear. In some cases, their clothing is left behind to show the person is no longer on earth. While some details of how we will ascend at the rapture are unclear, it is clear it will take place quickly, leaving many wondering what took place.

However, the second coming will present a strong contrast. Jesus will return visibly to earth to judge His enemies. Matthew 24:23-27 describes a clear arrival of the Lord. Verse 27 says, "For as the lightning comes from the east and flashes to the west, so also will the coming of the Son of Man be." Everyone will know when the Lord arrives at the second coming. As eventful as Christ's arrival was in Jerusalem on Palm Sunday, it will not compare with the ultimate triumph with which He will arrive at the end of the tribulation.

Suddenly

Similar to the rapture, the second coming will take place suddenly. Revelation 3:3 states, "I will come upon you as a thief, and you will not know what hour I will come upon you." In Matthew 24:44, Jesus also warned His disciples in the parable of the watchful homeowner, "Therefore you also be ready, for the Son of Man is coming at an hour you do not expect." This is true not only of the rapture but of the return as well in regard to the unsaved. In both instances, unbelievers will remain unexpectant of the Lord's coming.

Dramatically

In addition to coming suddenly, Christ will return at His second coming dramatically. Matthew 24:29 teaches, "Immediately after the tribulation of those days the sun will be darkened, and the moon will not give its light; the stars will fall from heaven, and the powers of the heavens will be shaken." As mentioned earlier, these signs will take place as part of the Lord's return while the world is under severe judgment. The light of the sun and moon will not be visible, while the stars will appear as though falling. These dramatic signs will signal the time of the Lord's return.

Gloriously

The second coming will include Jesus returning gloriously. Matthew 24:30 describes Jesus as arriving with great power and glory. Second Thessalonians 1:7 predicts Jesus will return with His mighty angels. This will serve as a royal, splendid appearance that Paul calls a "glorious appearing." According to Titus 2:11-13:

> For the grace of God that brings salvation has appeared to all men, teaching us that, denying ungodliness and worldly lusts, we should live soberly, righteously, and godly in the present age, looking for the blessed hope and glorious appearing of our great God and Savior Jesus Christ.

Triumphantly

Ultimately, Jesus will return triumphantly. Revelation 19:19-21 speaks of the destruction of Christ's enemies and the victory He will win upon His appearing. Jesus triumphed over sin and death through His resurrection (Colossians 2:15). At His return, He will triumph again as He conquers His enemies and begins His millennial reign.

As dramatic and triumphant as the return of Christ will be, it effectively sets the stage for His millennial reign and the eternal state to follow. The marriage of the Lamb began the opening ceremonies in heaven. Now the King and His bride will rule for one thousand years on the earth as the devastated planet again blossoms like a rose. And you and I will be there.

7

THE MILLENNIAL KINGDOM: THE THOUSAND-YEAR REIGN

One of the most incredible prophecies in the Bible is the coming of the kingdom of Christ to the earth. Those of us who believe in the rapture are often criticized for being escapists who want to abandon the planet God created. In reality, nothing could be further from the truth. We actually believe we are coming back to reign with Christ for one thousand years during His millennial kingdom.

J. Richard Middleton, while not a pretribulationalist, calls for a "holistic vision of God's intent to renew or redeem creation." He calls this "the Bible's best-kept secret, typically unknown to most church members and even to many clergy, no matter what their theological stripe."[1] All too often most Christians simply assume that once you die and go to heaven, that's all there is to God's plan for your future.

More nonpremillennialists are beginning to recognize that the biblical picture of the future is not just otherworldly. The Hebrew prophets foresaw a time when the earth would be blessed and renewed during the messianic era (Isaiah 11:1-9; 65:17-25). In Matthew 19:28, Jesus referred to a "regeneration" (Greek *palingenesia*) or "renewal" (Greek, *palingensia*) that would come in the future. In Acts 3:21, Peter said that Jesus had been received up into heaven "until the times of restoration of all things, which God has spoken by the mouth of all His holy prophets since the world began."

Premillennialists of all types believe that a literal earthly kingdom is coming in the future when Christ the King returns. Therefore, Glen Kreider states, "Christian eschatology, the message of hope that one day God will complete His work of redemption, is necessarily optimistic...regardless of positions on the millennium."[2]

One of the unique features of biblical prophecy is the variety of ways the millennial promises have been interpreted.

Postmillennialists believe the church is the kingdom of God on earth. Therefore, it is the believer's responsibility to further the kingdom globally by preaching the gospel and enacting Christian laws, values, and principles until the whole world is converted to Christ. The thousand-year reign of Christ is interpreted symbolically as synonymous with the church age. Satan's power is viewed as being bound by the power of the gospel. Thus, the church is called upon to conquer unbelief, convert the masses, and govern society by the mandate of biblical law. Only *after* Christianity succeeds on earth will Christ return and announce that His kingdom has been realized.[3]

Amillennialists believe that things will get worse at the end of the church age. This approach sees no millennium of any kind on the earth. Most who hold this view tend to interpret the so-called millennial prophecies as being fulfilled in eternity. Biblical references to the "thousand years" are interpreted symbolically, and the church age ends with the return of Christ to judge the world and usher in eternity. God's promises to Israel are viewed as having been fulfilled in the church, the "New Israel," which replaces national Israel, for which they see no specific future. The church age is viewed as an era of conflict between the forces of good and evil, which culminates with the return of Christ.[4]

Premillennialists, like myself, believe Christ will return at the end of the church age *before* He sets up His literal kingdom on earth for a thousand years.[5] Most premillennialists also believe there will be a period of great tribulation on earth prior to the return of Christ. Some premillennialists believe the church will go through the tribulation (posttribulationalists). Others, like myself, believe the church will be raptured prior to the tribulation (pretribulationalists). Despite their differences in regard to the rapture of the church, premillennialists generally believe in the restoration of the state of Israel as setting the stage for the coming of Christ. We are convinced that the king must return before there can be a literal kingdom of God on earth.

The Kingdom of God

The older premillennial scholars distinguished between the *universal* kingdom of God and the *mediatorial* kingdom of God.[6] They understood the universal kingdom as an everlasting kingdom (Psalm 145:13) in which God reigns over the entire universe (Psalm 103:19). The mediatorial kingdom was viewed as the rule of God on earth through a divinely chosen representative who speaks and acts for God. In this regard the nation of Israel was viewed as a theocracy, directly ruled by God through the Davidic kings, but with the fall of Jerusalem to the Babylonians in 586 BC, the line of Davidic rulers came to an end.

The prophet Hosea predicted: "The children of Israel shall abide many days without king or prince" (Hosea 3:4). God Himself had departed from the ark of the covenant (Ezekiel 8–11). Yet, the prophets of Israel predicted the restoration of the Davidic line (Amos 9:11) when the Lord Himself would reign in Jerusalem (Isaiah 24:23).

Jesus said that the kingdom of God does not come in ways that can be observed in the church age (Luke 17:20). In other words, the church age is not a time of Jesus literally sitting on David's throne, ruling from Jerusalem with a rod of iron. That is yet to come during the earthly millennium.

Jesus is now on the throne of heaven (Revelation 5:6). He rules in the hearts of believers. It is a spiritual kingdom, in which the Spirit of God wants to transform our lives and make you and me citizens of the kingdom. So we have a dual citizenship right now. We are citizens of heaven, but we are also citizens of earth. But the Bible tells us there will come a time when Christ will return triumphantly to the earth, split the Mount of Olives in half, march through the eastern gate, and sit on

David's throne in Jerusalem. And He will rule the world with a rod of iron for a thousand years in a mediatorial messianic kingdom on earth.

The book of Revelation emphasizes this clearly. In Revelation 20, we read that Satan is bound in "the bottomless pit" for a thousand years. Then it says, those who knew the Lord and did not receive the mark of the beast ruled with Him for a thousand years (Revelation 20:4). Six times in this chapter, John uses the term "a thousand years." I think he wants us to get the idea that the kingdom will last a thousand years on earth.

This is a literal kingdom on earth, a theocracy, limited to a thousand years, in which God fulfills His promises to the Jewish prophets that He would one day bring the kingdom to Jerusalem and that the King would literally reign upon the earth. Jewish believers understand that. Those who have put their faith in *Yeshua the Mashiach*, Jesus the Messiah, understand as messianic believers that there has to be a future literal kingdom on earth to fulfill the promises of the prophets. The earthly rule is with a rod of iron, to rule those who are going to be born during the thousand years of that kingdom on earth.

Dwight Pentecost defines the premillennial view in his classic book *Things to Come* as:

> the view that holds that Christ will return to earth, literally and bodily, before the millennial age begins and that, by His presence, a kingdom will be instituted over which He will reign. In this kingdom all of Israel's covenants will be literally fulfilled. It will continue for a thousand years, after which the kingdom will be given by the Son to the Father when it will merge with His eternal kingdom. The central issue in this position is whether the Scriptures are to be fulfilled literally or symbolically. In fact, this is the essential part of the entire question.[7]

The Millennial Citizens

Who will be here during that time? We know that after the time of tribulation, the unbelievers will be judged because they have received the mark of the beast. They will come under the condemnation of the Lord Himself at His return (Revelation 19:11-21). But there are those who will have become believers during the time of the tribulation. Revelation 7:1-8 describes 144,000 Jewish people from the twelve tribes of Israel. It is obvious that they are Jews. The chapter then describes a whole host that nobody could number—a host of Gentiles who come to faith in Christ as well (v. 9). Many of them will survive the tribulation period and go on into the millennium.

That is why I believe the rapture has to take place before the tribulation period. The church-age believers are taken out before the time of wrath and tribulation. Those who are saved during the time of tribulation and survive will go into the millennial kingdom. If the rapture comes at the end of the tribulation and the church goes through the tribulation period, then all the believers are taken out at the end of the tribulation. In that case, there would be no believers left on earth in mortal bodies to populate the millennium!

So there have to be believers who survive the tribulation period, who are not part of the church. The church must be taken out first. Then comes the time of wrath and judgment as well as the conversion of the 144,000 Jews and an innumerable host of Gentiles. Then they and their descendants go into the millennium and live on earth during the thousand years, in which it is said by the prophet Isaiah, if somebody dies at one hundred, it will be like he was a child who did not live to full age (Isaiah 65:20). God will replenish the earth like the Garden of Eden. It will be like the days when people lived for hundreds of years in the book of Genesis.

Satan Bound

The millennial kingdom is not heaven. It is not perfect. But it is ideal. It is an ideal age of euphoria, in which Satan is bound for a thousand years. He is not just simply bound by the cross, in that he cannot steal your salvation. No, he is literally bound. Revelation 20:2 says the angel came down with a chain, laid hold of the dragon, that old serpent, the devil, and Satan and bound him for a thousand years. He cast him into the bottomless pit (the *abyss*, in Greek), shut him up, and put a seal upon him, that he could not deceive the nations any more until the thousand years were fulfilled.

Satan will be locked up, chained down, with the lid sealed. He cannot get out and deceive the nations. Satan is not bound in that sense today. Peter said he "walks about like a roaring lion, seeking whom he may devour" (1 Peter 5:8). Revelation 12:10 says he accuses the brethren day and night before the throne of God. There is deception and rebellion in the world today because Satan is still on the loose. When Jesus returns in triumph to set up His millennial kingdom for a thousand years, Satan will be locked away in the abyss.

Those who refuse to interpret Revelation 20 literally will ask: "Do you really think the chain is literal?" It is a real chain all right! It may not be made of iron, but whatever it is it can hold down the devil. To which we might ask: Is Satan real? Is the abyss real? Is the binding real? Of course they are! God will by His own sovereign power restrain Satan during the millennium. He cannot get out. He is not on a long chain. He is on a short chain, chained down, locked in, lid sealed, and cannot deceive the nations. Christ, the Redeemer, will rule the world from the throne of David, and the saints will reign and rule with Him.

Theocratic Kingdom

The prophets of Israel predicted a time when the nation of Israel would be so blessed of God, and the King of righteousness would reign and rule on earth. The prophet Isaiah said, "Your people shall all be righteous; they shall inherit the land forever" (Isaiah 60:21). It is literally a land promise for Israel. Jesus is pictured as the "Prince of Peace" (Isaiah 9:6-7), who will bring peace to the world during that thousand years of His millennial reign. He will reign in righteousness and holiness (Zechariah 14:20). Jeremiah said God will make a new covenant with His people (Jeremiah 31:31-34). The curse will one day be removed, and Jesus will reign and rule as a theocratic king.

In the church age, we do not have a theocracy. The church is never called upon to bring in the kingdom of God on earth. Only the King can bring in the kingdom. We are never going to have a literal theocracy this side of the millennium. All such attempts in history have ended in a disaster, whether they begin in Geneva, London, or Boston. They never work, because fallible people are trying to produce an infallible society. It cannot be done. Only the Savior Himself, Jesus Christ, the Son of God, can produce such a kingdom. And one day, He will.

What will it be like? The prophet Daniel foresaw it. Notice what Daniel tells us about that great kingdom that is coming in the future:

> I was watching in the night visions,
> And behold, One like the Son of Man,
> Coming with the clouds of heaven!
> He came to the Ancient of Days,
> And they brought Him near before Him.
>
> (Daniel 7:13)

The "Ancient of Days" is the symbolic picture of God the Father. This does not mean that He is an old man. It means that He is the Eternal One. All of a sudden God, the Son of Man, comes before God, the Ancient One, to receive a kingdom.

> Then to Him was given dominion and glory and a
> kingdom,
> That all peoples, nations, and languages should serve
> Him.
> His dominion is an everlasting dominion,
> Which shall not pass away,
> And His kingdom the one
> Which shall not be destroyed.
>
> (Daniel 7:14)

There will come a time when Christ comes before the Father, and the Father gives Him the kingdom. But in His own parables, Jesus made it clear this occurs at the second coming. It is not at the first coming. He said in one of the parables that He would go away to a far country (heaven); He would be gone for a long time (nearly two thousand years now); and when He finally returned, it would be after having received the kingdom in heaven from the Father (Luke 19:11-27).

Jesus is in heaven preparing a place for the believers and receiving that kingdom. He is getting ready to rapture the church home to heaven, to the judgment seat of Christ, to the marriage of the Lamb, and for the triumphal return, when He rides out of heaven as the warrior King in triumph. He not only defeats the enemy, the Antichrist. But he binds Satan in the abyss for a thousand years, and sets up His kingdom on earth, where He will literally reign and rule on David's throne.

That has not happened yet; it will happen in the future. Jesus rules in the hearts of believers, but He is not literally ruling the world today. Satan is still the god of this world. He still wanders about like a roaring lion, seeking whom he may devour (1 Peter 5:8). There is still trouble, difficulty, tragedy, war, conflict, and deception in the world in which you and I live. We are not yet in the millennial age. That is yet to come.

The proof of that is simply asking the question, "Are there people deceived today?" Absolutely. They are deceived by false religions and false cults. They have not come to real faith in Jesus as their Savior, as Lord and Messiah of their lives. That deception will cease only when Christ returns and literally rules the world with a rod of iron.

Saints Reign

The time of the reign of Christ will include the raptured church that will reign and rule with Him (Revelation 19:14). The resurrected saints of the tribulation period will reign and rule with Christ as well (Revelation 20:4). The living saints who have survived the tribulation, the believers, will go into the millennial kingdom. The generations that they will produce during the thousand years will also be part of the kingdom. While the believers in glorified bodies reign and rule, those in natural bodies live out life on earth, because it is a time of utopia, euphoria, and prosperity, of feast and blessing. There will be no deception. The devil is not there. He is bound in the abyss.

The Savior Rules

Notice again three key elements of the millennial kingdom. First, Satan will be bound. There will be no deception and no war. It will be a time of peace and prosperity on the planet. Second, the saints will reign and rule with Christ. And third, the Savior rules the world.

If Jesus is really the Son of God, and He rules from heaven, why is it necessary for Him to rule on earth? It is to fulfill the prophecies of the Old Testament prophets. Otherwise, they are false prophecies. For example, Amos said, "On that day..." That always refers to some *future* day. It is not this day right now (Amos's day), but "that day" in the future. "On that day I will raise up the tabernacle of David, which has fallen down" (Amos 9:11).

Amos was not talking about singing David's music. He was talking about David's kingdom, which the northern tribes had rejected in Amos's time. The dynastic line of the kingdom of David would fall in 586 BC. The house of David would be all but destroyed by the Babylonians. The kings would be removed. Yet Amos foresaw a time when a Davidic King would rule in the future. The descendant of that line is Jesus Himself.

> "Behold, the days are coming," says the LORD,
> "When the plowman shall overtake the reaper,
> And the treader of grapes him who sows seed;
> The mountains shall drip with sweet wine,
> And all the hills shall flow with it."
>
> (Amos 9:13)

In other words, you cannot plant the crop fast enough because of the great harvest that will come in that future day.

> "I will bring back the captives of My people Israel;
> They shall build the waste cities and inhabit them;
> They shall plant vineyards and drink wine from them;
> They shall also make gardens and eat fruit from them.
> I will plant them in their land,
> And no longer shall they be pulled up

From the land I have given them,"
Says the LORD your God.

(Amos 9:14-15)

This is a promise to the nation and people of Israel to have a literal kingdom in the future. But it is not just the Jewish people going back with self-determination, saying, "We're going to do it." They will never do it without the help of God. No, speaking through Ezekiel the prophet, God said they will have to be regenerated: "I will give you a new heart and put a new spirit within you; I will take the heart of stone out of your flesh and give you a heart of flesh." And through the prophet Jeremiah, God adds:

"Behold, the days are coming," says the LORD,
"That I will raise to David a Branch of righteousness;
A King shall reign and prosper,
And execute judgment and righteousness in the earth.
In His days Judah will be saved,
And Israel will dwell safely;
Now this is His name by which He will be called:
THE LORD OUR RIGHTEOUSNESS."

(Jeremiah 23:5-6)

The prophet Zechariah said, "In that day a fountain shall be opened for the house of David and for the inhabitants of Jerusalem, for sin and for uncleanness" (Zechariah 13:1).

All this has to happen in order to bring about a literal kingdom on earth that is a kingdom of righteousness, where Ezekiel's vision of a future temple will finally be restored. Why? To demonstrate God's holiness and to provide a dwelling place for the glory of God. Just as the glory of God rested on the cherubim of the ark of the covenant, and just as the glory of God was in the place of the Holy of Holies, so when God returns to earth, when Christ comes to reign and rule, the glory returns. It will return to the millennial temple described in Ezekiel 40–48.

That is the place that will house the glory of God. That is where the holiness of God will be on display, and Christ will sit on David's throne, reigning and ruling over the world. What a day that is going to be! And the book of Revelation tells us how long it is going to last—for a thousand years.

The church age is of yet-unspecified length. It began on the Day of Pentecost. It will end on the day of the rapture. But then, the kingdom, when Christ returns, will be a thousand years long. Christ will be seated on the throne of David, in the city of Jerusalem, and reign and rule on the earth with a rod of iron. The nations will come to Him for justice and for judgment, and He will govern the world.

The center for divine government in the future will not be in the White House. It will be in God's house. That is when we finally have the fulfillment of these prophecies. That is when the culmination comes. The Savior who went to the cross to suffer and die, rose from the dead, and ascended back into heaven, will one day come in the rapture to call the church home to heaven. He will take us to the judgment seat of Christ, take us to the marriage, and then bring us back in the triumphal return, to reign and rule with Him on earth.

Oh, what a day that will be—when Jesus is literally here, and His nail-scarred hands shout to the world, "I love you. I did it all for you!" He is not coming back just to crush unbelief. He is coming back to encourage the faith of the believers, to grow that faith into a blessing of God for a thousand years.

The blessings that America has had all these years, that we do not even deserve, are nothing compared to the blessings of Christ ruling the entire world, when there is no war, no conflict, no terrorism, no sin, and no deception. Oh, there will be unregenerate people. But they will not be in charge. Christ will reign and rule this world.

And as wonderful as that millennial kingdom is, that is still not the end. For ultimately, He will deliver that kingdom up to the Father, and reign and rule forever in all eternity. And you and I will have the privilege of ruling with Him, not just upon the earth, but in eternity, over the expanse of the universe.

What's So Great About the Millennial Kingdom?

With all the emphasis on the various views and what will take place during this thousand-year reign, you might be wondering, *What's so great about the millennial kingdom?* From the perspective of the premillennial view, there will be much to celebrate for believers in Christ.

Future Evangelism

Following the massive judgments of the tribulation period and the destruction of God's enemies at Armageddon, Christ's millennial reign will offer an unprecedented time of peace, including spiritual peace during what will most likely serve as the greatest harvest of souls in human history. Tim LaHaye describes the encouragement of this future time:

> It is most encouraging to realize that many times more people will be converted during the millennial Kingdom than will be lost. Because the millennial population will undoubtedly exceed the total world population during the whole of biblical history, and since the majority living at that time will be Christian.[8]

With Jesus ruling the world in person, the free and unhindered spread of the gospel will be unprecedented. Millions will be converted. Schools, hospitals, and public services will be Christian. While people will still have to make their own decision for Christ, there will be no false religion or satanic opposition to dissuade them.

Future Rewards

In addition to future evangelism, we will experience future rewards. Believers will literally experience the opportunity to rule and reign with Christ during this period. For example, in 1 Corinthians 6:2-3, Paul refers to our future reign with the Lord:

> Do you not know that the saints will judge the world? And if the world will be judged by you, are you unworthy

to judge the smallest matters? Do you not know that we
shall judge angels? How much more, things that pertain
to this life?

"Saints" encompasses all believers, including you as a follower of
Jesus. Do you realize you will help judge the world? When will this take
place? During the millennial kingdom. This is the first time believers
will reign with the Lord in this world before the creation of the new
heavens and new earth.

Further, we will even judge or lead angels. This fascinating note
does not receive much attention in Scripture, but points to a future
reality beyond our full understanding. Faithful believers will lead other
people and even spiritual forces in the future.

John refers to our future millennial reign earlier in Revelation as well:

And he who overcomes, and keeps My works until the end,
to him I will give power over the nations—

"He shall rule them with a rod of iron;

They shall be dashed to pieces like the potter's vessels"—

as I also have received from My Father; and I will give
him the morning star.
(Revelation 2:26-28)

The Old Testament passage referred to here is found in Psalm 2:9:

You shall break them with a rod of iron;
You shall dash them to pieces like a potter's vessel.

The context of this Psalm speaks of the Messiah's future reign over His
kingdom—a kingdom we will reign over with Him.

The apostle John also sees tribulation saints, those who come to
faith in Jesus during the tribulation period, as ruling with Christ in
the millennial kingdom. He sees thrones and those seated on them
to whom the ability to judge will be given. This is similar to Daniel
7:9-10. Since Jesus promises the apostles they would sit on thrones
to judge the twelve tribes of Israel, it seems likely this promise will

take place during the millennial kingdom as well (Matthew 19:28; Luke 22:29-30).

Regarding how these rewards will operate in the millennial kingdom, John MacArthur says:

> Heaven will not involve differing qualities of service, because everything heavenly is perfect. Everything done for the Lord will be perfectly right and perfectly satisfying. There will be no distinctions of superiority or inferiority, and there will be no envy, jealousy, or any other remnant of sinful human nature. Whatever one's rank or responsibility or opportunity, those will be God's perfect will for that individual and therefore will be perfectly enjoyed. In a way that is beyond our present comprehension, believers will be both equal and unequal in the Millennium and in the eternal state.[9]

Future Covenant Fulfillment

Part of the millennial kingdom's importance will be to fulfill the biblical covenants God has made throughout history. Four unconditional covenants God has made with Abraham and the Jewish people are:

- The Abrahamic Covenant: God's promise to bless Abraham's descendants (Genesis 12, 15)

- The Land Covenant: God's promise for an eternal reign from Israel (Deuteronomy 30)

- The Davidic Covenant: God's promise for David's eternal kingdom reign (2 Samuel 7:12-16)

- The New Covenant: God's promise to include Gentile believers in the Messiah in His kingdom (Jeremiah 31:31-34)

Many aspects of these covenants require the Messiah's future reign from

Jerusalem in Israel. This has not yet happened—and will not—until the millennial kingdom.

In his comments regarding what the millennium will mean for Christ, Charles Ryrie makes the following important observation:

> Why is an earthly kingdom necessary? Did He not receive His inheritance when He was raised and exalted in heaven? Is not His present rule His inheritance? Why does there need to be an earthly kingdom? Because He must be triumphant in the same arena where He was seemingly defeated. His rejection by the rulers of this world was on this earth (1 Cor. 2:8). His exaltation must also be on this earth. And so it shall be when He comes again to rule this world in righteousness. He has waited long for His inheritance; soon He shall receive it.[10]

The millennial kingdom is essential in fulfilling the long-awaited promises and inheritance of our Lord and Messiah Jesus Christ.

Future Millennial Temple

Did you know there will be a temple in the millennial kingdom? There is a temple described in Ezekiel chapters 40–48 that is distinct from the temple that will exist during the tribulation period. This final temple will exist in Jerusalem as the place where Christ is worshipped on earth.

A full description of this temple and its courts is given in Ezekiel 40:1–44:31. No such building as Ezekiel so minutely describes has ever been built. His prophecy cannot refer to either Zerubbabel's or Herod's temple. Since there is no temple in the New Jerusalem (Revelation 21:22), this must be a description of the temple that will be on earth during the millennium. That it does not belong to the new earth is also clear from Ezekiel's mention of seas and deserts and other locations that will not be found on the new earth after its renovation by fire.

The new temple will lack many things that were part of the old temple. There will be no ark of the covenant, no pot of manna, no

Aaron's rod, no tablets of the Law, no cherubim, no mercy seat, no golden candlestick, no showbread, no veil, no unapproachable Holy of Holies. Jesus will be a King-Priest and perform the duties of high priest conjointly with His kingly office.

Why will a temple exist during the millennial kingdom? Charles Dyer offers two important reasons:

> (1) The sanctuary was the visible symbol of God's presence among His people. The prelude to Israel's judgment began when God's glory departed from Solomon's temple in Jerusalem (Ezek. 8–11). The climax to her restoration as a nation will come when God's glory reenters the new temple in Jerusalem (43:1–5). (2) The new temple will become the visible reminder of Israel's relationship to God through His New Covenant. This temple will be the focal point for the visible manifestation of Israel's new relationship with her God.[11]

Though church age believers may not understand the importance of a physical temple, the Jewish perspective has long viewed the temple as a vital part of worshipping the Lord God. What will take place in this final temple? Prophecy expert Ron Rhodes explains:

> This temple will be a worship center of Jesus Christ during the entire millennium. It will be built at the beginning of the messianic kingdom (Ezekiel 37:26-28) by Christ (Zechariah 6:12-13), redeemed Jews (Ezekiel 43:10-11), and representatives from the Gentile nations (Haggai 2:7; Zechariah 6:15).[12]

The prophet Ezekiel describes this future millennial temple as the location of God's dwelling place:

> Moreover I will make a covenant of peace with them, and it shall be an everlasting covenant with them; I will establish them and multiply them, and I will set My sanctuary in their midst forevermore. My tabernacle also shall be with

them; indeed I will be their God, and they shall be My people. The nations also will know that I, the LORD, sanctify Israel, when My sanctuary is in their midst forevermore (Ezekiel 37:26-28).

Jews and Gentiles together will worship Jesus in perfect harmony during this period.

Future Worship

This future millennial temple will also include worship of the Lord Almighty. According to Ezekiel's description, one key aspect of this worship will be a reinstitution of the temple sacrifices. Though these sacrifices are not required in the current church age (Hebrews 7–10), they will once again operate at the Messiah's temple during the millennial kingdom and serve as memorials of Christ's atoning death for our sins. Lamar Cooper writes:

> The millennium will afford Israel the opportunity for the first time in its history to use the symbols of their covenant with Jesus as Messiah in view. It will be their first time to be a kingdom of priests and a holy nation showing forth to the world the redemptive work of Yahweh in the person of Jesus Christ the Messiah (Isa 53:7; 61:1-3; Zech 4:1 [*sic* 3:10]; John 1:29; Acts 8:32-35; 1 Pet 1:19; Rev 7:13-14; 5:9; 13:8; 15:3).[13]

Why will God include temple worship and sacrifices during the millennial kingdom? Merrill Unger notes from Ezekiel the following four important purposes:

1. to demonstrate God's holiness (42:1-20)

2. to provide a dwelling place for the divine glory (43:1-17)

3. to provide a center for the divine government (43:7)

4. to perpetuate the memorial of sacrifice (43:18-27)[14]

Rhodes also notes the reason for these sacrifices may include the need "to remove ceremonial uncleanness and prevent defilements from polluting the purity of the temple environment."[15]

Future Global Prosperity

The worldwide conditions of the millennium will allow the unprecedented growth of global prosperity. There is no reason to believe that this world will go back to a time when there was no exponential technology growth. The conditions on earth under the rule of King Jesus will be conclusive for an explosion of technology the likes of which the world has never seen. The world's greatest physicians, scientists, doctors, engineers, teachers, and laborers will use technology for the good of mankind and the universe under the Lord's guidance. The failed attempt of a global system under the Antichrist will stand in sharp contrast to the successful reign of King Jesus.

Future Earthly Redemption

We often talk about the curse on our world, but did you know five curses took place in the Garden of Eden (Genesis 3:14-19)? These include curses against the serpent, Satan, Adam (representing all men), Eve (representing all women), and nature. The millennial kingdom will offer an opportunity to redeem creation from these curses.

For example, the curse against the serpent, representing animals, will be changed. Animals will live in peace, with the wolf and lamb living together in peace (Isaiah 11:6-9). The curse against Satan will differ from our current time as he will be locked away from activity until one final rebellion at the end of the millennium. Instead of times of increased evil and temptation, the world will enjoy peace and freedom from Satan's attacks during the millennial reign.

The curse against men and women will also change. Just as people lived for an extended time before the flood in Noah's day, the death of a person who is one hundred years old will be considered a premature death (Isaiah 65:20). God will heal the sicknesses and diseases of His people (Isaiah 33:24). While those of us raptured will be living in our glorified bodies, those who were alive in natural bodies after the tribulation as believers will live in a time of unprecedented peace and health.

The curse against nature will also be removed. Isaiah often speaks of the abundance of food and natural resources that will exist in the millennial kingdom (30:23-25; 35:1-2; 62:8-9). The scarcity of food, water, and other resources will no longer be issues under the millennial reign of our Savior Jesus Christ. Wars will be eliminated allowing the earth to blossom and prosper. Isaiah 2:4 expresses this future blessing when the nations will "beat their swords into plowshares." Global peace will prevail for a thousand years.

The Conclusion of the Millennial Kingdom

As wonderful as the millennium will be, it will not be heaven. Despite the amazing period of blessing and prophetic fulfillment in the millennial kingdom, this time will be sandwiched between two important conflicts. Prior to the millennial kingdom, Satan and his forces are defeated by Jesus at Armageddon. At the end of the millennial kingdom, Satan is released for one final rebellion. Revelation 20:7-10 describes this battle:

> Now when the thousand years have expired, Satan will be released from his prison and will go out to deceive the nations which are in the four corners of the earth, Gog and Magog, to gather them together to battle, whose number is as the sand of the sea. They went up on the breadth of the earth and surrounded the camp of the saints and the beloved city. And fire came down from God out of heaven and devoured them. The devil, who deceived them, was cast into the lake of fire and brimstone where the beast and the false prophet are. And they will be tormented day and night forever and ever.

These words reveal several key details of the millennial kingdom:

1. Satan will be imprisoned during this time but not yet cast into the lake of fire.

2. Nations will continue to exist during the millennial kingdom.

3. People will continue to sin during this time, including rebellion in this final battle against Jesus and His kingdom.

4. God will quickly defeat His enemies and cast Satan into the eternal lake of fire.

5. This battle will be followed by the great white throne judgment of unbelievers before the creation of the new heaven and new earth (Revelation 20:11–21:5).

Who are those who will battle against God's people? John Walvoord suggests those who follow Satan will include:

> Those who survive the Tribulation will enter the Millennium in their natural bodies, and they will bear children and repopulate the earth (Isa. 65:18-25). Under ideal circumstances in which all know about Jesus Christ (cf. Jer. 31:33-34), many will outwardly profess faith in Christ without actually placing faith in Him for salvation. The shallowness of their professions will become apparent when Satan is released. The multitudes who follow Satan are evidently those who have never been born again in the millennial kingdom.[16]

What will this battle include? Satan and his enemy army will surround Jerusalem. The battle will be short-lived. God's fire will destroy His enemies and Satan will be cast into the lake of fire forever. Like Armageddon in Revelation 19:11-21, this so-called battle will actually serve as an execution. As Satan's forces move in for the attack, "fire came down from God out of heaven and devoured them" (20:9). They will be instantly destroyed. Satan's forces will be physically killed, and their souls will enter the realm of punishment, awaiting their final sentencing to the lake of fire, which will take place in the upcoming judgment (20:11-15).

The devil who deceived them "was cast into the lake of fire and brimstone" (20:10). There he will join the beast and the false prophet, who by that time will have been in that place of torment for a thousand years (19:20). Those sentenced to that terrible place will be "tormented day and night." There will not be a moment of relief. Scripture explicitly teaches their punishment is eternal. The same Greek phrase translated "forever and ever" is used in Revelation 1:18 regarding Christ's eternity. Believers are already citizens of God's kingdom (Philippians 3:20), blessed to be in the King's family and fellowship. A glorious future inheritance awaits us that is "incorruptible and undefiled and that does not fade away, reserved in heaven for you" (1 Peter 1:4).

Many people have neglected the study of the millennial kingdom, dismissing it as confusing or unimportant in comparison with the future new heaven and new earth. However, the millennial kingdom offers yet another Bible prophecy that serves as part of the amazing future we will enjoy with Christ. As my friend Mark Hitchcock observes, "The Millennium is no optional part of God's plan for the end times. It must occur for God to keep His promises."[17]

Further, we should *long* for this time, knowing we will live and even reign with the Lord in a world far better than the one we live in today. We need not fear this future time. Rather, we should anticipate the millennial kingdom with great joy, knowing our Lord will use it to fulfill His promises to rule the earth.

8

THE NEW HEAVENS AND NEW EARTH: SPENDING ETERNITY WITH GOD

The closer we get to heaven, the more we want to know about our future home. While all believers will be in the Lord's presence immediately after this life ends (Philippians 1:20), we also grow in anticipation of heaven as we mature in both our walk with God and in physical years. Some of my dearest friends who have gone before me have lived their last earthly days meditating on what God's Word teaches about heaven. In some ways, it reminds me of people who look at the brochures of the scenic destinations for their upcoming trip. They want to know everything possible before they arrive. While the pictures in the advertisements help, they rarely compare with the beauty of a location like the Grand Canyon or the Rocky Mountains.

In his classic work titled *Heaven*, Randy Alcorn suggests:

> Spiritually speaking, we live in the country of the Blind. The disease of sin has blinded us to God and Heaven, which are real yet unseen. Fortunately, Jesus has come to

our valley from Heaven to tell us about His father, the
world beyond and the world to come.[1]

As we read the concluding chapters of Revelation, we are immediately swept into the grandeur of a brand-new world. Even the blessings
of the millennium do not compare. It is beyond human imagination.

Scripture offers us an exciting, though limited, look at our future
destination. After the thousand-year millennial kingdom, during
which our Lord Jesus reigns upon His throne from Jerusalem, Satan
will make one final stand. However, his rebellion will not last long.
God will send fire to quickly end this attack (Revelation 20:9). Satan's
rebellion will end with the devil being cast into the lake of fire for
eternity future (Revelation 20:10). Mark Hitchcock explains this final
doom of Satan as having three parts: 1) Satan bound, 2) Satan released,
and 3) Satan defeated.[2]

Scripture then provides a glimpse of the great white throne judgment (Revelation 20:11-15). This event will include "the dead, small
and great, standing before God" (v. 12). While believers will already be
with the Lord, this judgment will include every unbeliever, those who
perished apart from saving faith in Jesus Christ. These unbelievers will
be judged by their works (v. 13), indicating there will likely be some
variation or degree of punishment in the lake of fire.

This final judgment prepares the way for all that God has prepared
for His people. The Bible's closing two chapters provide information
in five key areas regarding eternity future to encourage believers today.

Destruction of Current Heaven and Earth

Revelation 21 begins with the glorious prediction of the old heaven
and earth passing away, being replaced by a new heaven and earth. This
refers to the atmospheric heaven, not the third heaven. The dwelling
place of God does not need to be replaced. The last two chapters of
the Bible describe this glorious place in detail and provide an account
of what it will be like. While this may not sound like good news, the
destruction of the current heaven and earth reflects the fulfillment of
many biblical passages.

Psalms

For example, the psalmist noted in Psalm 102:25-26:

> Of old You laid the foundation of the earth,
> And the heavens are the work of Your hands.
> They will perish, but You will endure;
> Yes, they will all grow old like a garment;
> Like a cloak You will change them,
> And they will be changed.

The Jewish people had long understood that the Lord would one day replace the brokenness of this world with a renewed existence, calling both the old and new heaven and earth the "work of Your hands."

Isaiah

The prophet Isaiah also described this event:

> All the host of heaven shall be dissolved,
> And the heavens shall be rolled up like a scroll.
>
> (Isaiah 34:4)

Isaiah predicted this sign as part of both God's future judgment and as a precursor to a new existence in the Lord's presence. In 13:13, Isaiah notes God's plan to "shake the heavens, and the earth will move out of her place." In 51:6, Isaiah describes the Lord's prediction regarding the new heavens and earth:

> Lift up your eyes to the heavens,
> And look on the earth beneath.
> For the heavens will vanish away like smoke,
> The earth will grow old like a garment,
> And those who dwell in it will die in like manner;
> But My salvation will be forever,
> And My righteousness will not be abolished.

The prophet repeatedly associated God's salvation with the new heaven and earth, connecting the hope of the believer with eternal community in the presence of the Messiah.

Jesus

Jesus similarly described the passing of our current heavens and earth, noting, "Heaven and earth will pass away, but My words will by no means pass away" (Matthew 24:35). His teaching included the promise of judgment upon the current world along with equating His own words with those of the Lord. His words are eternal, just as the words of God are described by the psalmist in Psalm 119 and elsewhere in the Old Testament. Robert Jeffress writes, "One of the most remarkable aspects of our worship in heaven will be seeing Jesus face-to-face. Our response to that experience will be unlike anything we've ever known on earth."[3]

Peter

The apostle Peter builds upon both the teachings of the Old Testament and Jesus with the reminder of the day of the Lord: "But the day of the Lord will come as a thief in the night, in which the heavens will pass away with a great noise, and the elements will melt with fervent heat; both the earth and the works that are in it will be burned up" (2 Peter 3:10).

Some dispute whether the new heaven and earth will be remodeled or completely remade. Some argue the earth will simply be re-created or reformed for the new heavens and earth. For example, W.A. Criswell suggests, "The elements shall return to their primordial form, and that whole creation of God shall be burned with fire (2 Peter 3:10, 12). It shall be cleansed. It shall be purged. Everything that is wrong and everything that is transgressing and sinful shall be taken out of it."[4]

David Jeremiah similarly states: "Rather than being totally annihilated, the present heaven and earth will be cleansed, glorified and equipped for our eternal use...All the ingrained evidence of decay wrought into the earth's crust, especially the fossils and the cemeteries and all other monuments belonging to the long march of death will be completely destroyed."[5]

William Hendricksen views this ultimate rejuvenation as nature's wonderful self-realization when it is no longer subject to futility and arrested development because of human sin. He writes, "Thus it is with the present universe, which lies under the curse...What a glorious day it will be when all restraints which are due to sin will have been removed."[6]

Others, however, argue a completely new heavens and earth is more likely. Not only will the current world be burned up, passed away, and made new, but this new heaven and earth reflects a parallel with the first creation. Just as God created the heavens and earth from nothing in the beginning (Genesis 1:1), He will create a new heaven and earth free from sin and death where we will dwell with Him for all eternity.

John Walvoord writes:

> Scriptures are strong in their statement of the destruction of the old heaven and old earth...In view of the tremendous energy locked into every material atom, the same God who locked in this energy can unlock it and destroy it, reducing it to nothing...it is possible that the destruction of the physical earth and heaven will be a gigantic atomic explosion in which all goes back to nothing.[7]

Strong arguments have been made for both views. Regardless, the biblical passages appear to indicate a complete renovation or recreation with its focus on the glorious new world that is coming.

Creation of the New Heaven and Earth

While the Bible's final two chapters provide the most details regarding the new heaven and earth, four biblical passages address this topic. Let's look at the other three passages and then investigate what Revelation 21 describes.

Isaiah 65:17

Isaiah's description of eternity future includes the words,

> "For behold, I create new heavens and a new earth;
> And the former shall not be remembered or come to
> mind."

Taken literally, those in eternity future will no longer dwell upon the past but will enjoy the experience of everlasting joy with the Lord and His people.

The following verses in Isaiah 65 add to the description, emphasizing a new Jerusalem (v. 18) where people rejoice with no more weeping or crying (v. 19).

Isaiah 66:22

Isaiah's second passage regarding the new heavens and earth compare eternity future with the future of God's people. Just as the new heavens and earth will endure forever, God's people will live for eternity:

> "For as the new heavens and the new earth
> Which I will make shall remain before Me," says the
> LORD,
> "So shall your descendants and your name remain."

These comforting words should be viewed with joy. Sometimes a person will ask, "What will we do in heaven? Sitting around singing forever sounds boring." However, this is an inaccurate perspective. Instead of boredom, take the closest moment you've ever experienced with the Lord, multiply it by one billion, and extend that moment with no ending. Even this exaggerated measure will not even compare with the amazing future every moment will provide for us in our eternal presence with our Savior.

2 Peter 3:13

When the apostle Peter addressed the topic of God creating the new heavens and earth, he looked forward to the time with great anticipation: "Nevertheless we, according to His promise, look for new heavens and a new earth in which righteousness dwells." Peter emphasized the promise, the anticipation, and God's righteousness.

The promise Peter shared built upon the prophets of the Old Testament as well as the teaching he personally received from Jesus. Peter taught that these promises would literally be fulfilled. Just as Peter had personally experienced Jesus bring about the completion of many prophecies through His death and resurrection, he spoke with confidence regarding the remaining unfulfilled aspects of Bible prophecy related to the last days.

Revelation 21:1

The apostle John began his description of the new heaven and earth with the words, "Now I saw a new heaven and a new earth, for the first heaven and the first earth had passed away. Also there was no more sea." Two important observations can be noted. First, John emphasized the end of the previous heaven and earth. The world of sin and brokenness would be replaced by a perfect existence led by its creator and king.

John MacArthur says: "Think about this: Heaven is where holiness, fellowship with God, joy, peace, love and all other virtues are realized in utter perfection." He suggests that all the qualities of the fruit of the Spirit will characterize heaven because "we have the life of God in us. And the rule of God over us."[8]

Second, the new heaven and earth will have "no more sea." Prophecy expert John Walvoord notes the importance of this comment:

> In contrast with the present earth, which has most of its surface covered by water, no large body of water will be on the new earth. The Bible is silent, however, on any features of the first heaven except the statement in 21:23 that there will be no sun or moon and, by implication, no stars. The new heaven refers not to the abode of God, but to the earth's atmosphere and planetary space.[9]

While the creation of the first heaven and earth were "good," the new heaven and earth will be perfect. What began in the Garden of Eden will end in a new heavenly city. The original creation of man and woman in fellowship with God will transition to all God's redeemed people dwelling in community with Him forever. The entire family of God will be there: Old Testament saints, New Testament saints, tribulation saints, and millennial believers. Beyond the great tribulation and the millennial kingdom lies the final reality: the eternal state. There is a powerful reminder in the closing chapters of the Bible that this present world is not the end. There is indeed a new world coming where God dwells among us.

Bruce Metzger writes:

> Whether John would have us think of the new heavens and new earth as a transformation of the existing order, or whether the present cosmos will come to an end and a new creation replace it, is not quite clear. In any case, the word *new* used by John does not mean simply another but a new kind of heaven and earth.[10]

Description of the New Heaven and Earth

John's description of the new heaven and earth includes an emphasis on three areas: the holy city, God's presence, and perfect righteousness. Eternity future will include a perfect place, a perfect presence, and a perfect plan prepared for a perfect people who will live forever in a final state of eternal sinless glorification within the perfect love of God.

Bernard Ramm expressed it beautifully when he wrote:

> The curtain of revelation drops with a final vision of glorification. The glorified shall reign for ever and ever. It is a *reign!* That is, it is a condition of complete glorification… a perfect sharing in the wonder of God. And it is *eternal.* It will last forever and ever…knowing an existence free from all pain, death, and mourning, and knowing an existence only of happiness, bliss, joy and glory without end.[11]

The Holy City

We will discuss the New Jerusalem more in the next section, but here we'll simply note two things. First, the New Jerusalem represents a holy city. While Jerusalem has served as the capital of God's Jewish people in Israel for three thousand years, it serves as only a shadow of the perfect city of eternity future.

Second, the New Jerusalem represents God's first priority in the new heavens and earth. It is talked about before the mention of God's presence or the removal of sin. We should be encouraged by the emphasis God gives toward creating an eternal location where we will forever live with Him.

Twelve is the biblical number of totality or completeness. We can see multiples of twelve in the administration of God's universe. There are twelve tribes of Israel and twelve apostles. There are twenty-four elders seated on twenty-four thrones (a double twelve) around the altar and 144,000 witnesses (twelve times twelve thousand) (Revelation 14), who will probably gain special leadership positions during the millennial kingdom.

Many references to twelve are seen in this picture of the New Jerusalem that will come down from heaven (Revelation 21:9-21):

Twelve gates. Twelve entrances will always be open for God's people to have access to the New Jerusalem. Revelation 21:12-13 indicates there will be three gates on each of the four sides of this gigantic city. The twelve gates will resemble twelve gigantic pearls.

Twelve angels. Again we see the relationship of angels in the eternal order and their work with the human race. They are pictured standing at the twelve gates (Revelation 21:12), presumably to guard access and welcome the children of God.

Twelve tribes. Each of the twelve gates has the name of one of the tribes of Israel written on it, indicating that the children of Israel will have ready access to this splendid heavenly city that will house the redeemed of all time. Since angels are mentioned, it seems that each of the tribes has its angel, just as each of the churches in Revelation 2–3 has its angel.

Twelve foundations. The foundation walls of the city will be magnificent beyond comprehension. In verses 19-21 they are described as "adorned with all kinds of precious stones."

And John says in verse 16 that the city "is laid out as a square"; it is as wide as it is long as it is high. It is like a gigantic cube about fourteen hundred miles wide and high and deep. It would quite easily accommodate the billions of people who have come to know Christ as their personal Savior over the centuries. All the family of God is there.

Then John tries again to describe the indescribable. He uses the analogy of precious stones, and lists and names all the stones, many of which were found on the breastplate of the high priest of Israel. Those stones then symbolize this great city that is coming in the future. Then John says in verse 22, "But I saw no temple in it."

An overview of the description of this city reveals:

1. Splendor: like a jasper, clear as crystal (Revelation 21:11)
2. Wall: 144 cubits (220 feet) high (verse 17)
3. Gates: giant pearls named for the twelve tribes of Israel (verses 12,21)
4. Measurement: foursquare—fourteen hundred—mile cube (verse 16)
5. City itself: pure gold, like clear glass (verse 18)
6. Street: pure gold, like transparent glass (verse 21)
7. Temple: God and the Lamb are the temple (verse 22)
8. Light: glory of God and the Lamb (verse 23)
9. Nations: those who are saved (verse 24)
10. Access: gates that are never closed (verse 25)
11. Activity: no night there (verse 25)
12. Purity: none who defile (verse 27)

Regarding the measurements of the city, Robert Mounce offers an insightful description of verse 16:

The city that appears to John is said to lie "foursquare" (NRSV). This could mean that it was laid out in a square pattern, but more likely it refers to a three-dimensional form—a cube whose length, breadth, and height are all equal. Not only are the terms in which the city is described most naturally interpreted as a cube...This particular shape would immediately remind the Jewish reader of the inner sanctuary of the temple...the place of divine presence. A city foursquare would be the place where God has taken up residence with his people.[12]

The biblical measurements equal a cube about 1,500 miles wide, long, and high. It will be large enough to house a hundred thousand million. There will be no physical temple there because God and the Lamb (Christ) are the temple (Revelation 21:22). David Jeremiah observes, "Many people believe the city of New Jerusalem will be like an immense Holy of Holies, which serves as the dwelling place of God in the temple of His new universe."[13]

God's Presence

Revelation 21:3 notes, "Behold, the tabernacle of God is with men, and He will dwell with them, and they shall be His people. God Himself will be with them and be their God." John's use of the word "tabernacle" is interesting. The Jewish people constructed a tabernacle in the wilderness under the command of Moses as a place of worship. In the new heaven and earth, God will no longer dwell above the tabernacle but will dwell with His people.

The mention of "bride" in verse 2 is also important. The church is called the bride of Christ throughout the New Testament. Believers (the bride) in the New Jerusalem will come to meet Christ (the bridegroom), reflecting the wedding traditions of Jewish culture. All believers will be involved in this event, from the biblical heroes like Abraham and Moses to believing family members who have gone before us as we dwell forever in the Father's house.

Today, as believers we experience God's presence in our lives through the Holy Spirit's indwelling work. However, in our future existence we will enjoy His presence as an all-encompassing experience with the Lord directly in our midst. We will "see His face" (Revelation 22:4) and have an audience with the King regularly.

Our Heavenly Existence

David Jeremiah offers a compelling description of our future heavenly existence in the New Jerusalem:

> When we get to the new heaven and the new earth, the curse will be reversed. It will be lifted; it will be dispelled forever. Oh, think of it! The weariness that accompanies our work will be a forgotten memory. Nature will work as it should, the weather will always be in our favor, and the ground will grow flowers as naturally as it produces thorns and thistles today. We ourselves will not fall into the ground in death because we will never die.[14]

In fact, Revelation offers many "no more's" we will enjoy.

Twelve "No More's" of the New Heaven and Earth

No more...

- sea (21:1)
- death (21:4)
- tears (21:4)
- sorrow (21:4)
- crying (21:4)
- pain (21:4)
- unbelievers (21:8)
- temple (21:22)
- sun or moon (21:23; 22:5)
- night (21:25; 22:5)

- sin (21:27)

- curse (22:3)

A.T. Pierson adds:

> There shall be no more curse—*perfect restoration.* The throne of God and of the Lamb shall be in it—*perfect administration.* His servants shall serve him—*perfect subordination.* And they shall see his face—*perfect transformation.* And his name shall be on their foreheads—*perfect identification.* And there shall be no night there; and they need no candle, neither light of the sun; for the Lord giveth them light—*perfect illumination.* And they shall reign forever and ever—*perfect exultation.*[15]

Capital of the New Heaven and Earth

The new heavenly city will have no temple. John says, "And I saw no temple in it, for the Lord God Almighty and the Lamb are its temple" (Revelation 21:22). Several passages affirm that there is a temple in heaven (Revelation 3:12; 7:15; 11:19; 15:5). Here, it is clear there is none in eternity. How can this be? The temple is not a building; it is the Lord God Himself. Verse 23 continues the thought of no temple except God and the Lamb: "The city had no need of the sun or of the moon to shine in it, for the glory of God illuminated it. The Lamb is its light." The glory of God that illuminates all heaven defines it as His temple. There is no need for a temple in the eternal state since God Himself will be the temple in which everything exists. The presence of God literally fills the entire new heaven and new earth (see 21:3). Going to heaven will be entering the limitless presence of the Lord. We will be dwelling there with Him and in Him in His presence.

The earthly temple kept the high priest out of the Holy of Holies except on the Day of Atonement. It kept the other priests limited to the Holy Place, and kept the laymen limited to the courtyard. In heaven, no one will be limited. Everybody will have access into the presence of God Himself.

In these closing chapters of Revelation, the Lamb (Christ) rules with God the Father in the throne, in the temple, and in the holy city. We see that the Son is co-equal with the Father. The emphasis is on the deity of Christ throughout these passages. And Revelation 21:24 tells us who is going to be there: "And the nations of those who are saved shall walk in its light, and the kings of the earth bring their glory and honor into it."

Randy Alcorn adds, "The city's open gates are a great equalizer. There's no edition in Heaven; everyone will have access because of Christ's blood. His death is the admission ticket to every nook and cranny of the New Jerusalem."[16]

Only the saved will enter the New Jerusalem. Only the saved will be in the new heaven and the new earth. Only the saved will participate in the family of God for all eternity. John also tells us who is not going to be there. He gives a long list of people in 21:8. The list includes the unbelieving, the abominable, murderers, immoral persons, sorcerers, idolaters, and liars. In other words, those who have never been saved, whose hearts have never been transformed, and whose eternal destiny has never been changed will not be there.

The good news is, anyone who wants to come into the presence of God in heaven may come. The final invitation of Scripture is, "Whoever desires, let him take the water of life freely" (Revelation 22:17). But the bad news is, those who do not choose to come, those who do not put their faith and trust in Christ, will be excluded. They will not be there. All the lost and unsaved will not be there.

The saved of the nations will be there in heaven for all eternity. The promise is a promise to every believer. All of those whose names "are written in the Lamb's Book of Life" will be there (Revelation 21:27). Knowing that your name is written down in heaven, in the Book of Life, is what secures your eternal destiny in heaven itself.

In chapter 22, John continues his description. "He showed me a pure river of water of life, clear as crystal, proceeding from the throne of God and of the Lamb." And then in verse 2, "In the middle of its street, and on either side of the river, was the tree of life." That has not appeared in the Bible since the third chapter of Genesis, when Adam and Eve were banished from the Garden of Eden. The tree of life is the symbol that Paradise is regained in the heavenly city, in the Holy Place, in the heavenly temple. There, the people of God have access to the presence of God, to the life of God, and to the power of God. In every sense the New Jerusalem is paradise regained. It is a city that looks like the Garden of Eden.

Randall Price also observes:

> God's new creation (Revelation 21:5) bears many similarities with His original creation. The inner city has "a river of water of life," "the tree of life," and "fruits" and "leaves… for healing of the nations" (Revelation 22:1-2). Although reminiscent of the Garden of Eden (Genesis 2:8-17), there is no reason to suppose the scene in either narrative is symbolic. Like the earthly Tabernacle and Temple, which were patterned after the heavenly originals, the earthly Garden of Eden could have been created as an archetype of the New Jerusalem.[17]

The New Jerusalem is described in the Bible as ultimately the highest heaven. The apostle Paul said in 2 Corinthians 12:2 that he was "caught up to the third heaven." He was not referring to the atmosphere around the planet, the clouds, or even outer space, but to the dwelling place of God, the third heaven. That is the place being described for us here in the book of Revelation.

John may be speaking of the stones, jasper, gold, and gates of pearl to literally describe the city. Or he may be trying to use human language to describe the indescribable, something that is beyond our anticipation or recognition. But the most important thing is stated in Revelation 22:3—"And there shall be no more curse." The curse of sin is gone. The curse of death is removed.

In addition, "The throne of God and of the Lamb shall be in it, and His servants shall serve Him. They shall see His face" (Revelation 22:3-4). "They shall see His face" was an idiom used in the first century, when John wrote this, to refer to having an audience with the king. The average person never saw the king face-to-face. If you had an audience with the king, you had an opportunity to literally look right into his face. You would see his face. John is saying to us that in heaven, we will regularly have an audience with the King. We will see His face. The very face of God finally will be revealed to believers for all of eternity.

John also tells us in verse 3 that there is a purpose for us being there. We are going to be God's servants. We will serve Him forever. We are not just floating around endlessly in heaven. We are busy serving the Lord. And verse 5 says, "And they shall reign forever and ever." The eternal reign of the believer is pictured here in the New Jerusalem. We are going to be busy serving God. We are going to be reigning and ruling with Him over the vast expanse of the universe that is already beyond our human reach and comprehension. God is giving us just a glimpse of what is out there. Ultimately, we are going to see it all. We are not going to need a rocket of any sort to get us from one universe to another, from one experience to another. No, we will have time and opportunity to do it all, to see it all, and to experience it all.

People often think, *I need to travel and see the world*. People have their bucket list of the many things they wish to do before they die. Let me assure you, there are millions and millions of things to do for all eternity, when we will never die. That is the promise of the Bible. Eternal life is the gift of God. Those who live forever will serve Him forever. They will reign with Him forever. They will be there forever. What a promise!

As John wraps up the book of Revelation, Jesus says to us: "I am the Alpha and the Omega, the Beginning and the End, the First and the Last." John adds, "Blessed are those who do his commandments, that they may have the right to the tree of life, and may enter through the gates into the city" (Revelation 22:13-14).

Then the whole book of Revelation comes down finally in the end to an instruction and an invitation. Jesus Himself speaks: "I, Jesus, have sent My angel to testify to you these things in the churches. I am the Root and the Offspring of David, the Bright and Morning Star" (Revelation 22:16). Jesus instructs us, "Preach this in the churches." He personally commands that prophecy serve as an important part of the church's teachings. To avoid this is to fail to proclaim the whole counsel of God. It is to fail the people of God by robbing them of their glorious hope of their eternal future.

John then closes with these words of invitation: "And the Spirit and the bride say, 'Come!' And let him who hears say, 'Come!' And let him who thirsts come. Whoever desires, let him take the water of life freely" (Revelation 22:17). These words clearly indicate the evangelistic purpose of God's revelation. He has shown us the future so that He may call us to faith in Himself. He is our ultimate eternal destiny.

People of the New Heaven and Earth

Revelation 21:24 mentions "the nations" or literally "the peoples." This means the redeemed people from every nation and ethnic group will dwell in heaven's light. In the eternal city, there will be no more divisions, barriers, or exclusions because of race or politics. All kinds of people in eternity blend into the people of God, and they will move freely in and about the eternal city.

Somebody asked me one time, "Ed, do you think there will be anything manmade in heaven?" I think the answer to that is "Yes!" If nothing else, the nail prints in Jesus' hands and feet were still there after the resurrection. He showed the disciples the nail prints to convince them it was really Him (Luke 24:40). Those nail prints will shout to us for all eternity, "I love you! I love you! I love you! I did it all for you."

I've enjoyed fellowship with believers in nations all over the world. When two Christians have Jesus in common, it doesn't matter how many differences we have socially, ethnically, or racially. We are one in Christ. We have unity in Him automatically. When Jesus in you meets Jesus in another believer, there's an immediate connection. Times of Christian fellowship are wonderful. The rest of the world doesn't know anything like it. But as wonderful as that fellowship is here and now, it cannot compare to the perfect fellowship we will have in the eternal city.

Imagine what it will be like to live in the community of the redeemed. In our final glorified state there will be no sin, no death, no heartache, no jealousy, no competition. We will all live for the blessing of everyone else and for the glory of God. In the heavenly Jerusalem all the hopes and dreams of earth will finally be realized.

In the meantime, may we live on this earth as citizens of heaven, confessing that we are pilgrims. We seek a city that is eternal in the heavens, whose builder and maker is God, looking to Jesus the author and finisher of our faith (cf. Hebrews 11:13-16; 12:2).

9

THE FINAL PICTURE: FUTURE GLORY!

The final chapter of Revelation indicates the eternal city will be returned to the inherent qualities of the Garden of Eden—only on a grander scale. Then, and only then, will the Creator's true intention for humanity finally be realized. There in the center of the New Jerusalem, John the revelator sees the *river of life* flowing from the throne of God and the Lamb (v. 1). It is the source of all life that emanates from God Himself. Then John sees something that has been missing from the Bible since Genesis 3—*the tree of life*!

Paradise will be restored in the holy city. The biblical story of the human race begins in the garden and ends in the eternal city. In between stands the cross of Jesus Christ. He alone has changed the destiny of the human race.

The river of life is reminiscent of the river of Eden whose tributaries flowed in four directions (Genesis 2:10-14). The tree of life (Genesis 2:9) bears twelve types of fruit and is perpetually in bloom. The beautiful picture painted by the words of this chapter remind us that the best of the natural world will be preserved in the eternal world.

Yet Revelation 22, the Bible's final chapter, offers more than a description of eternity future. Jesus offers additional words regarding our prophetic future (Revelation 22:6-11) and a final testimony

(Revelation 22:12-21). The opening section emphasizes a call to believers, while the second portion calls out to unbelievers. There is both a glorious eternal future for those who know the Lord, and eternal punishment and separation from God for those who reject Him.

The Lord emphasizes once again the time of His coming (22:6-11) and the testimony of His coming (22:12-21). Both aspects offer hope and warning for those living today.

The Time of Christ's Coming (Revelation 22:6-11)

The words of Revelation 22:6-11 emphasize the time is always near. Three times the promise is repeated: "I am coming quickly" (vv. 7,12,20), which means "soon" or "suddenly." It points to the imminent return of Christ. There is no doubt, regardless of one's eschatological views, that the reader of Revelation is left awaiting and anticipating the coming of Christ at any moment. These teachings can be summarized in four parts: a time to obey (vv. 6-7), to worship (vv. 8-9), to proclaim (v. 10), and to serve (v. 11).

A Time to Obey (22:6-7)

In verses 6-7 we read:

> Then he said to me, "These words are faithful and true." And the Lord God of the holy prophets sent His angel to show His servants the things which must shortly take place.
>
> "Behold, I am coming quickly! Blessed is he who keeps the words of the prophecy of this book."

These words closely reflect the opening words of Revelation 1:1-3. The words of the angel emphasize the contents of Revelation as coming from Jesus, revealing what will take place in the future, and offering a blessing to those who obey its message.

The words are "faithful and true" because they are inspired by the Lord. John emphasizes that these words originated from the same God who sent the holy prophets of the Old Testament. This may also help explain why Revelation relies heavily upon Old Testament citations.

One writer observes, "Of the 404 verses in the book of Revelation, seemingly 278 of them make some allusion to the Old Testament. That is 68.8% of the verses!"[1] Another adds: "The book of Revelation contains citations from, or allusions to, 28 of the 39 books of the OT."[2]

These words offer the strongest authority possible. They include references to the Father, Jesus, the angels, the holy prophets, and the writings of the apostle John. Obeying these words should certainly include a blessing upon our lives! Yet many Christians, churches, and even entire denominations have often avoided a healthy focus on the words of Revelation. One commentator summarizes:

> Two opposite reactions seem to be prominent among Christians across the centuries. Some have become so infatuated with the book of Revelation that the remainder of the Bible has become little more than a support system for eschatology. The opposite reaction to that has been to view the book of Revelation as such a difficult book to understand as to render it worth little more than an occasional read. The vast majority of pastors make no attempt to teach their people the Apocalypse; and whenever pastors do choose to preach from the book, the messages usually end at chap. 3. In between these two extremes is the appropriate place where the book is carefully expounded and its treasures enshrined in the hearts of the people for whom the eschaton becomes a blessed hope as people are called to look for the appearing of the Lord.[3]

A Time to Worship (22:8-9)

John also realized the overwhelming greatness of the message before him, as well as the messenger angel in his presence. His response:

> Now I, John, saw and heard these things. And when I heard and saw, I fell down to worship before the feet of the angel who showed me these things.
>
> Then he said to me, "See that you do not do that. For I am

your fellow servant, and of your brethren the prophets, and
of those who keep the words of this book. Worship God."

The angel responded to John in three ways. First, the angel commanded John not to worship him. Those who claim we are to pray to
angels or worship them in any way find a clear rebuttal in these words.
Angels are the messengers of the Lord, not divine beings we are to bow
before in worship.

Second, the angel notes he is a fellow servant. The angel is a servant alongside John, not above him. In addition, angels are servants to
the prophets. The same messengers who brought God's words to Isaiah, Jeremiah, Daniel, and others are the same beings who revealed this
message to John. Even more amazing, these same angels are *our* fellow servants—if we keep the words of this book. In other words, the
angels serve alongside faithful believers to help us fulfill the purposes
of the Lord.

Third, the angel reminds John to worship God. We do not worship angels, we serve alongside angels, and with the angels we worship
our Lord. He is the only one worthy of all our praise. That is why all of
heaven, including the angels, fall down to worship the Father in Revelation 4 and worship Christ, the Lamb, in Revelation 5. In both cases
only the Father and the Son receive worship (Greek, *axios*, "worthy")
because they are holy (Greek, *hagios*).

A Time to Proclaim (22:10)

In addition to obedience and worship, we are called to proclaim the
words of God. Verse 10 shares the angel's message: "And he said to me,
'Do not seal the words of the prophecy of this book, for the time is at
hand.'" The Bible, including the words of Revelation, are not a secret
to hide but a message to share.

Unfortunately, many churches will not even address Bible prophecy. Reasons vary. Some pastors do not know prophecy very well, while
others find it divisive or confusing. Yet too much of Scripture consists
of prophecy to avoid it. Scripture is adamant that we are called to proclaim God's Word, including prophecy as noted here in Revelation. It

is part of "the whole counsel of God" (Acts 20:27) that we are expected to study, proclaim, and apply today. Whatever one's viewpoint may be, a proper understanding of biblical prophecy should motivate us to "[love] His appearing" (2 Timothy 4:8).

A Time to Serve (22:11)

The final verse in this section says, "He who is unjust, let him be unjust still; he who is filthy, let him be filthy still; he who is righteous, let him be righteous still; he who is holy, let him be holy still." Some have erroneously viewed the first part of this passage as condoning the sinful actions of the unjust in some fatalistic manner. However, nothing could be further from the truth. Thomas Constable notes:

> This is a strong warning to unbelievers, not to put off becoming a believer in Jesus Christ. It presents the *hopelessness* of the final state of unbelievers. When Christ comes, people will not be able to change their destiny. What they are then, they will remain forever! People should not expect some second chance in the future (after the Rapture), but should make the decision about worshipping (trusting in) God now, in the light of what they have read in this book (cf. Matt. 25:10; Luke 13:25; Heb. 9:27).[4]

The biblical mandate to evangelize the world and make disciples of all nations is clearly emphasized in Jesus' final words (Matthew 28:18-20; Mark 16:15; Luke 24:46-48; Acts 1:8). The believer's marching orders are clearly given throughout Scripture. Also, we are to keep serving the Lord until He comes (Matthew 24:46; Luke 19:13). God is on display to the watching world through our lives. What we say must be backed up by what we do. We are to be the Lord's "witnesses" (Greek, *marturia*) everywhere and at all times.

We cannot delay in receiving Christ for salvation, nor should we delay in faithful daily living in anticipation of His coming. We cannot receive the blessings of keeping the words of this book if we live in selfishness and rebellion to the Lord.

The Testimony of Christ (Revelation 22:12-21)

While Revelation 22:6-11 reminds us the time of Christ is near, the remainder of Revelation's final chapter concludes with one final testimony that consists of seven parts: a reward (vv. 12-13), blessing (v. 14), judgment (v. 15), invitation (vv. 16-17), warning (vv. 18-19), reminder (v. 20), and conclusion (v. 21).

A Reward (22:12-13)

These two brief verses offer two sections that each consist of three parts. Verse 12 says, "And behold, I am coming quickly, and My reward is with Me, to give to every one according to his work." The first promise is that Jesus is "coming quickly" (Greek, *tachu*, "suddenly"). The emphasis is on the fact that He will come rapidly and without warning. While we have waited nearly two thousand years already, "quickly" is written from the perspective of the author of time. To Him, a day is like a thousand years (2 Peter 3:8). When Jesus does return to rapture His bride, He will do so instantly, in the "twinkling of an eye" (1 Corinthians 15:52). Thus, every generation of believers must live their lives as though Jesus could come at any moment—and one day He will!

In the second part, Jesus says, "My reward is with Me." What does He mean by this? The greatness of our eternal rewards is based on the Giver of the gifts. When our gifts come from Jesus, we know they are perfect and true. The same principle is true in this life. When a person receives a gift, it is often considered more valuable when it is given by someone considered important.

Consider the medals given at the Olympic Games. The gold medal is valuable because of the value of precious metals. However, it is considered far more valuable because it is presented by the organizers of the Olympic Games to athletes who have proven themselves to be the best in the world in a particular event. When we receive our eternal rewards from Jesus, their value will be of infinite worth because they come from the King of kings and Lord of lords.

Third, verse 12 tells us that Jesus will give to each person according to their work. While our salvation is by grace alone through faith alone, our rewards are based upon our service. We cannot believe in Jesus and then do nothing and expect great honors in eternity. God has a plan for each of our lives and expects us to "be transformed by the renewing of your mind, that you may prove what is that good and acceptable and perfect will of God" (Romans 12:2).

Verse 13 also consists of three unique parts. First, Jesus calls Himself "the Alpha and the Omega." This phrase is used only of Jesus and only in Revelation a total of four times (1:8,11; 21:6; 22:13). Alpha and omega are the first and last letters of the Greek alphabet, the language used to write Revelation and the other books of the New Testament. Jesus is the start and end of all things, who was with God in the beginning and is God (John 1:1-3).

Second, Jesus calls Himself "the Beginning and the End." Just as every good story or film has a strong introduction and conclusion, Jesus serves as the author of the story of life. He is creator, sustainer, and the one who will reign victoriously for eternity future. Revelation 1:8 adds, "'the Beginning and the End,' says the Lord, 'who is and who was and who is to come, the Almighty.'"

Third, Jesus calls Himself "the First and the Last." He uses the same phrase in Revelation 1:11 just before commanding John to write down the letters to the seven churches. Because Jesus is the first and the last, He has authority over all creation and over the church, including each of us as believers. We are called to submit to His authority in our lives. He gives us His love while also providing us purposes to fulfill, both in this life and in eternity.

A Blessing (22:14)

The second area Jesus notes is a blessing. Verse 14 says, "Blessed are those who do His commandments, that they may have the right to the tree of life, and may enter through the gates into the city." This blessing begins similarly to the Beatitudes Jesus gave in the Sermon on the Mount in Matthew 5. Here, only one directive is associated with God's blessing—obeying God's commands.

Those who obey receive two privileges in eternity future. First, we will "have the right to the tree of life." This tree of life was first mentioned in Genesis where it was found in the Garden of Eden (2:9; 3:22-24). Proverbs mentions "a tree of life" as a blessing (3:18; 11:30; 13:12; 15:4). Only Revelation speaks again of the tree of life as a physical object. Revelation 2:7 promises access to the tree of life to those who overcome, a term that includes all believers.

Revelation 22:2 offers the main description of the tree of life. It will be located on the new earth in the New Jerusalem: "In the middle of its street, and on either side of the river, was the tree of life, which bore twelve fruits, each tree yielding its fruit every month. The leaves of the tree were for the healing of the nations." This tree offers life, productivity (fruit), and healing. Since there is no disease or death in eternity, the idea of the tree is that it is health-giving as a source of life in the eternal state.

Those who have the right to this tree will "enter through the gates into the city." This city is the New Jerusalem. Every believer will one day have access to this new eternal city where the main joy will consist of living in the presence of the Lord, His angels, and His people forever and serving Him in His vast universe.

A Judgment (22:15)

In contrast with the blessings of those living in eternity with the Lord is a judgment upon unbelievers: "But outside are dogs and sorcerers and sexually immoral and murderers and idolaters, and whoever loves and practices a lie." This sevenfold judgment addresses key sinful actions that are representative of all sin apart from the forgiveness provided through Christ. The term *dogs* was used in biblical times to refer to unbelievers.

Those who experience judgment do so because they willfully rejected the Lord. Just as the rich man recognized his wrong in eternal torment (Luke 16:24-28), so also others who are rejected from eternity with God will realize they have received their proper judgment.

However, no one is worthy of God's sinless presence by his or her own merit. Apart from the Lord's grace through salvation, all people sin and fall short of God's glory. This explains why we will bow in worship before God. We know we are not there because we deserve it, but because of His grace and mercy.

An Invitation (22:16-17)

The final appeal of verse 16 comes directly from the mouth of Jesus. Just as many letters in ancient times concluded with a personal word from the author, our Lord names Himself in His parting words to the church that conclude the New Testament. He states, "I, Jesus, have sent My angel to testify to you these things in the churches. I am the Root and the Offspring of David, the Bright and Morning Star."

Again, Jesus refers to Himself with three names—Jesus, the Root and Offspring of David, and the Bright and Morning Star. Jesus indicates His role as Savior. As the offspring of David, He fulfills the prophecies as the coming Messiah. As the morning star, Jesus refers back to Revelation 2:28, noting the connection between the believers who will be with Him and His role as the leader of eternity.

Verse 17 shifts to a focus on the Holy Spirit. The invitation is threefold: the Spirit and the bride say "Come," and whoever wishes may come.

The bride (the church), along with the Holy Spirit, offers an invitation to the hearers of Revelation. Just as Jesus invited people to salvation during His earthly ministry, He continues to invite unbelievers to follow Him through His revelation and through His people who minister in this world. This includes you and me! We are part of the bride of Christ, those expected to share the good news and help others find this water of life.

This is why Jesus left this world giving us the Great Commission (Matthew 28:18-20). Why are we still in this world as believers? God has a plan for our lives that includes bringing His love and hope to every person possible. We are not only to live pure as the bride of Christ; we are to take as many people to heaven with us as we can.

A Warning (22:18-19)

Fifth, Jesus offers a stern warning to those who would tamper with the words of Revelation:

> For I testify to everyone who hears the words of the prophecy of this book: If anyone adds to these things, God will add to him the plagues that are written in this book; and if anyone takes away from the words of the book of this prophecy, God shall take away his part from the Book of Life, from the holy city, and from the things which are written in this book.

Why such harsh words to conclude a section highlighting the glories of eternity future with the Lord? Hitchcock explains:

> This means that the inspired canon of Scripture was closed at the end of the first century when Revelation was finished. Therefore, any false prophet, counterfeit, or charlatan who adds alleged new revelation to it will face divine vengeance. This is a sober warning to all the cults that add to God's Word and to all the critics who take away from God's Word by denying the inspiration of Scripture and cutting out the supernatural events within it.[5]

The blessings of eternity future include a stern warning. Those who change the message will not receive the positive future in the message. Those who change God's words today, whether in Revelation or other parts of Scripture, do so in one of the ways John explains.

First, some false teachers add to God's words. For example, the Book of Mormon claims to be additional revelation from Jesus Christ. While Mormons accept the Bible, they add more to the biblical revelation, often contradicting it.

Second, some false teachers take away from God's words. Some have applied this warning to the teachings of the Jehovah's Witnesses because of its New World Bible that changes the translation of the names of God and changes other passages (particularly John 1:1) to match its theology, which denies the deity of Christ.

However, this same warning could be applied to other Christian movements that no longer use the Old Testament or use only certain feel-good parts of Scripture to present a version of Christianity that is different from what is found in the full counsel of God's Word. The warning also applies to how we approach the book of Revelation itself. Faithful preachers of this book should not try to make it say more than it says nor less than it says. We must be careful neither to add to or take away from Scripture, even the parts that are difficult to understand, as we seek to honor the Lord. As Wiersbe explains:

> In John's day, books were copied by hand, and the copyist might have been tempted to edit or emend the material. Even today, people add their theories and traditions to God's Word or strike from it whatever does not fit into their scheme of theology. John's warning applied specifically to the Book of Revelation, but certainly it includes all of the Word of God.[6]

The wise servant of the Lord neither adds to nor subtracts from the inspired words of God (2 Timothy 3:16-17). Instead, we are called to hear them and practice them in our lives. J.A. Bengel is attributed as saying, "Apply yourself to the whole text, and apply the whole text to yourself."[7] Other Christian leaders throughout history have based their lives upon accepting and obeying God's Word as it has been revealed:

> "Nobody ever outgrows Scripture; the book widens and deepens with our years."—Charles Spurgeon

> "The Word of God I think of as a straight edge, which shows up our own crookedness. We can't really tell how crooked our thinking is until we line it up with the straight edge of Scripture."—Elisabeth Elliot

> "The Bible is the book of my life. It's the book I live with, the book I live by, the book I want to die by."—N.T. Wright

"Oh, give me that book! At any price, give me the book of
God! I have it: here is knowledge enough for me. Let me
be: 'A man of one book.'"—John Wesley[8]

In the introduction of the Bassandyne Bible, the first Bible printed
in Scotland, we find these words that offer tremendous insight into the
high view of Scripture Christians are called to hold:

Here is the spring where waters flow,
To quench our heart of sin,
Here is the tree where truth doth grow,
To lead our lives therein.

Here is the judge that stints the strife,
When men's devices fail:
Here is the bread that feeds the life
That death cannot assail.

The tidings of salvation dear,
Comes to ears from hence:
The fortress of our faith is here,
And shield of our defense.

Then be not like the swine that hath
A pearl at his desire,
And takes more pleasure from the trough
And wallowing in the mire.

Read not this book in any case,
But with a single eye:
Read not but first desire God's grace,
To understand thereby.

Pray still in faith with this respect,
To bear good fruit therein,
That knowledge may bring this effect,
To mortify thy sin.

Then happy you shall be in all your life,
What so to you befalls:

Yes, double happy you shall be,
When God by death you calls.[9]

A Reminder (22:20)

Sixth, Jesus offers one final reminder of His return: "Surely I am coming quickly." These words connect with 3:11, where we read, "Behold, I am coming quickly! Hold fast what you have, that no one may take your crown." Despite the persecution faced by the early church in Philadelphia and other locations, the anticipation of His soon return helped fuel their faithfulness during difficult times.

The apostle John then offers his own words of reflection as part of this final reminder he identifies himself as one who witnessed the visions of Revelation, saying, "Amen. Even so, come, Lord Jesus!" The word *amen* means "yes" or "so be it." John fully agrees with God's plan to return suddenly. Though John did not live to see the rapture, he lived exiled on Patmos where the thought of soon being in the Lord's presence forever offered a glorious alternative to the struggles of his earthly life.

The request, "Even so, come," connects with verse 17. Just as the Spirit, the bride (the church), and him who hears say, "Come," John wholeheartedly agrees that we are to anticipate that the Lord will suddenly come to receive us. His emphasis on "Lord Jesus" is also important. Though common throughout the New Testament, the final two verses of Revelation include the only two times the title "Lord Jesus" is used in the book. John concludes using the strongest words possible to acknowledge Jesus as far more than a rabbi who lived in Israel during the first century. This teacher who healed the sick, gave sight to the blind, and rose from the dead now reigns in heavenly glory.

A Conclusion (22:21)

The last verse of Revelation offers our seventh aspect of Christ's testimony, a conclusion focused on the grace of Jesus: "The grace of our Lord Jesus Christ be with you all. Amen." We often forget Revelation was originally composed to circulate among churches for public reading. English audio recordings of Revelation are generally around an hour and fifteen minutes in length. As the reader concluded the reading of Revelation in early church services, the listeners would be reminded of the grace of the Lord Jesus Christ.

This is only the second of two uses of the word *grace* (Greek, *charis*) in Revelation, 1:4 being the other. We could say that Revelation is bookended by God's grace, which encompasses all.[10] Spurgeon poetically preached:

> Whatever you may miss, may the Grace of our Lord Jesus Christ be always with you. In whatever points you, or any of us may fail, may we never come short of the Grace of our Lord Jesus Christ!...May it be with us transfiguring us from glory to glory till we shall bear the image of Jesus Christ![11]

In Revelation, as in the Gospels, grace has the first and last words. It is the expression of God's love that draws us to the Savior and keeps us in His presence. This is the message of Scripture, beginning in the garden, where humanity had a direct relationship with God, to the concluding words to His people who will dwell in relationship with Him in the city of God. We will no longer exist as one man and one woman near the tree of life. We will be Christ's bride, the family of God, living with the Lord at the tree of life for all eternity. This will be our *future glory* and what a glorious and amazing future this will be!

10

WHY YOUR FUTURE MATTERS TODAY

The choices we make today determine what happens to us in the future. When I was a student in college, a girl I had dated only once in high school came home on spring break and sat right in front of me in church. I had not seen her for several years. But the Spirit of God prompted me to ask her for a date. That was the beginning of a lifelong relationship. Now, more than fifty years, three grown children and seven grandchildren later, it is obvious how God's plan has been working for our good through all the blessings and challenges of life.

The same is true of God's wonderful plan for our eternal destiny. As the apostle Paul said so confidently, "If God is for us, who can be against us?" (Romans 8:31). Grant Jeffrey, who is now in heaven, once wrote:

> The greatest adventure of man's history lies before us if we will only turn from our sin and accept God's offer of eternal life. The Word of God tells us that "the gift of God is eternal life in Christ Jesus our Lord" (Romans 6:23). We do not have to wait until we die to receive eternal life. The moment we accept Christ's pardon, we are transformed from spiritual death to eternal life.[1]

We are living in the most incredible times the world has ever known. Live reports via satellite beam the latest events from around the globe into our living rooms every day. For the first time in human history, technology has allowed us to watch global developments of great significance as they unfold before our eyes. Everything from political crises to international conflicts and global pandemics come to us live as they are happening around the world.

Many people believe we are living in the end times—an era when the world will be plunged into a series of cataclysmic disasters. Despite incredible medical, scientific, and technological advances, only an ignorant person could think that humans are clever enough to avoid a final confrontation of disastrous consequences. We may dodge the apocalyptic bullet a few more times, but sooner or later, we will have to face the final moment of history.

In light of this, the Bible has much to say about our eternal future. Whereas unbelievers face the hopelessness of eternity without God, believers have much to hope for. We know that one day Jesus will come to take us to the Father's house (John 14:1-3). Though our world continues to face much trouble, God has not revealed when the rapture will take place. We are called to live obedient to the Lord's commands until He comes. This was made clear to the disciples at the time of the ascension of Jesus. They asked Him if He was going to restore the kingdom to Israel at that time. Jesus answered, "It is not for you to know times or seasons which the Father has put in His own authority" (Acts 1:7).

Two observations are clear in this verse. First, the Father has already set the time. Second, we are not supposed to know the time. Instead, we have a role to fulfill until He takes us to live in the Father's house. In the next verse, Jesus states the Great Commission, saying, "But you shall receive power when the Holy Spirit has come upon you; and you shall be witnesses to Me in Jerusalem, and in all Judea and Samaria, and to the end of the earth" (Acts 1:8). Then, Jesus surprised them by ascending into the sky, leaving them staring at the clouds.

In verse 11, angels instruct the disciples, "Men of Galilee, why do you stand gazing up into heaven? This same Jesus, who was taken up from you into heaven, will so come in like manner as you saw Him go into heaven." We often find ourselves in a similar situation. We want to watch for the signs of Christ more than we want to serve Christ. The message of the angels can inform us still today. We are not called to worry about the timing of the rapture. He will return on His schedule at the perfect moment. Instead, the Lord calls us to several challenges as we await the fulfillment of His promises.

Why does God's future matter for us today? Scripture offers several reasons Bible prophecy impacts our lives in the here and now. Our lives should be different as the result of studying the end times for the following ten reasons.

Reason 1: Demonstrate the Character of God

First and foremost, God leaves us in this world for the time being to bring glory to Himself. The Westminster Shorter Catechism declares: "Man's chief end is to glorify God and enjoy Him forever." Commenting on this, J.I. Packer states, "All serious Christian thinkers acknowledge that glorifying God is at once man's divine calling and his highest joy, both here and hereafter."[2] Thus, every true believer has an eternal calling to glorify God. That calling begins at the moment of regeneration and continues for all eternity.

Francis Schaeffer referred to this process as demonstrating the character of God to the watching world. He said,

> The world has a right to look upon us and make a judgment...The final apologetic, along with the rational, logical defense and presentation, is what the world sees in the individual Christian and our corporate relationships together...But our calling is a different calling: it is to exhibit God and show His character, by His grace in this generation.[3]

The Great Commandment is found in Matthew 22:37-39 where Jesus said, "'You shall love the LORD your God with all your heart, with all your soul, and with all your mind.' This is the first and great commandment. And the second is like it: 'You shall love your neighbor as yourself.'" As we study through His prophecies the amazing future God has in store for us, we sense how close we may be to His return. This sense of anticipation should provide a desire to live completely for the Lord every moment of every day.

Paul also spoke of this way of life as being a living sacrifice. In the Old Testament, God expected His people to present a suitable animal sacrifice before Him at the tabernacle or temple. In the New Testament, we discover God wants us to present our lives before Him as an offering:

> I beseech you therefore, brethren, by the mercies of God, that you present your bodies a living sacrifice, holy, acceptable to God, which is your reasonable service. And do not be conformed to this world, but be transformed by the renewing of your mind, that you may prove what is that good and acceptable and perfect will of God (Roman 12:1-2).

John Witmer writes:

> Christians are believer-priests, identified with the great High Priest, the Lord Jesus Christ (cf. Heb. 7:23-28; 1 Peter 2:5,9; Rev. 1:6). A believer's offering of his total life as a sacrifice to God is therefore sacred service. In the light of Paul's closely reasoned and finely argued exposition of the mercies of God (Rom. 1–11), such an offering is obviously a desirable response for believers.[4]

Peter also spoke of how we are to live in response to teachings that the Lord will return soon: "Therefore, beloved, looking forward to these things, be diligent to be found by Him in peace, without spot and blameless" (2 Peter 3:14). In our relationships, our desire should be to live in peace and without regrets as we relate to those around us. To be without spot and blameless emphasizes purity. Just as the animal sacrifices used in the temple required one's best offering, our lives are to offer our very best in living fully for the Lord. The apostle John reminded believers: "We know that when He is revealed, we shall be like Him, for we shall see Him as He is. And everyone who has this hope in Him purifies himself, just as He is pure" (1 John 3:2-3).

Reason 2: Share Christ with Others

Jesus commanded His followers to serve as His witnesses from the next person they met to the last person on the planet. The Great Commission teaches, "Go therefore and make disciples of all the nations, baptizing them in the name of the Father and of the Son and of the Holy Spirit, teaching them to observe all things that I have commanded you; and lo, I am with you always, even to the end of the age" (Matthew 28:19-20). As the motto of one Christian college is, "From the first verse to the last person." Our goal must be to take the gospel to every tongue, tribe, and nation.

Did you know there are more than 7,000 languages spoken on our planet? Of the approximately 7,353 languages spoken today by 7.7 billion people, only 3,384 languages have some Scripture translated in them. While languages spoken by 6.9 billion people can potentially read God's Word in a known language, many live without the Word of God available in their own language. The current estimate by the Wycliffe Global Alliance reveals 252 million people do not have a single word of Scripture in their language.[5] While this sounds like significant progress, these statistics do not include many languages with only Bible portions. One in five people are still waiting for the full Bible in their own language.[6]

Further, many who now have God's Word in their language cannot read it. As many as half of the world's people are functionally illiterate or live in oral cultures.[7] There is a tremendous need for Bible translation and audio Bible distribution, and those of us who have both must fund and take the Bible to those who have yet to hear. Knowing that Jesus could come at any moment, it should motivate us to do all we can to help bring the gospel to the unreached.

In addition to taking the gospel to the world, we need to take the gospel across the street to our friends, relatives, and neighbors. While we can earn the right to be heard by our deeds, it takes words to communicate the gospel. That is why Paul said, "How shall they hear without a preacher?" (Romans 10:14).

Reason 3: Focus on What Is Eternal

One reason I love studying Bible prophecy is that it tells us where we will spend most of our lives! Our life in this world may last up to a century, yet this does not compare with the eternity that awaits us. However, many people spend more time planning their vacation than they do where they will spend the afterlife.

In Colossians 3:1-4, Paul places our lives in the proper perspective:

> If then you were raised with Christ, seek those things which are above, where Christ is, sitting at the right hand of God. Set your mind on things above, not on things on the earth. For you died, and your life is hidden with Christ in God. When Christ who is our life appears, then you also will appear with Him in glory.

Notice the emphasis these words have on our mind. We are to "set our mind." Why? Because we will soon be with the Lord. In sports, athletes often visualize themselves making the last-second shot or crossing the finish line first. This expectation helps prepare the athlete to physically perform at his or her highest level. Likewise, when we focus our mind on being with the Lord soon, we can live in victory as we seek to please the Lord in our daily lives.

Another important passage in this area is Paul's words in 2 Corinthians 4:17-18:

> For our light affliction, which is but for a moment, is working for us a far more exceeding and eternal weight of glory, while we do not look at the things which are seen, but at the things which are not seen. For the things which are seen are temporary, but the things which are not seen are eternal.

Paul contrasts our temporary pains and hardships with the wonderful blessings of eternity with God. Commentator David Garland notes:

Since the persecution affects only the outer nature that is wasting away, it is destined to pass and to be replaced by something far more glorious. On earth, our afflictions seem never ending while the more sublime moments seem to pass by in a flash. Looking at things from the vantage point of God's new aeon puts everything, including affliction, in its true perspective.[8]

When we face suffering in this world, whether from living out our faith or simply the frustrations of life in a fallen world, we can look ahead to a time when all will be made right and we stand in the presence of our holy, perfect Lord.

Reason 4: Give to God's Priorities

People don't often like to talk about money, but Jesus did not hesitate to discuss finances. Some have observed that Jesus spoke about finances more than He did about heaven. One of His key teachings regarding finances is found in Matthew 6:19-21:

Do not lay up for yourselves treasures on earth, where moth and rust destroy and where thieves break in and steal; but lay up for yourselves treasures in heaven, where neither moth nor rust destroys and where thieves do not break in and steal. For where your treasure is, there your heart will be also.

When we have a proper perspective on heaven and eternity, we can make better decisions about our finances. William Barclay notes, "All purely physical pleasures have a way of wearing out. At each successive enjoyment of them the thrill becomes less thrilling. It requires more of them to produce the same effect. They are like a drug which loses its initial potency and which becomes increasingly less effective."[9] Yes, we must pay bills and even taxes (Romans 13:7), but our focus should be on eternal treasures.

Paul adds in 1 Timothy 6:17-19 that our wealth can be used to do good and help others, in addition to storing up eternal rewards:

> Command those who are rich in this present age not to be
> haughty, nor to trust in uncertain riches but in the living
> God, who gives us richly all things to enjoy. Let them do
> good, that they be rich in good works, ready to give, will-
> ing to share, storing up for themselves a good foundation
> for the time to come, that they may lay hold on eternal life.

Money is not bad but trusting in it can be. God gives us money both to meet our own needs and to help with the needs of others. What are some ways God has called us to store up treasures in heaven with our resources? We can give to...

- our local church (2 Corinthians 8:1-5)
- the poor, hungry, and thirsty (Matthew 25:35)
- the sick (Matthew 25:36)
- the persecuted (Matthew 25:36)
- world outreach and missions (2 Corinthians 8:1-5)
- saving lives (Acts 2:44-45)
- extended family (1 Timothy 5:4-8)
- orphans and widows (James 1:27)

These are only some of the ways God has called us to impact lives now that also impacts eternity. The more we invest our lives in these kinds of areas, the more we truly store up treasures in heaven.

Reason 5: Remain Committed to the Church

A fifth way prophecy motivates us today should be in our commitment to the local church. In the Bible, the word *church* is used in three ways. First, the Greek word *ekklesia* could refer to an assembly of people of any kind. However, the New Testament generally uses it in one of two other ways. In some cases, the church refers to the entire body of Christ, including every believer in Jesus (Hebrews 12:22-23). In other cases, *church* is used in specific reference to a local group of believers (1 Corinthians 1:2). In fact, virtually all of Paul's letters were written to churches (e.g., churches of Galatia) or church leaders (e.g., Timothy).

The church was never referred to in Scripture as a building but as a body. It is not an organization but an organism. The church is a movement not a monument. It is a community not a cathedral. In the first church, the focus was on the people of God serving the will of God. A quick look at earliest believers in Acts 2:42-47 reveals:

> They continued steadfastly in the apostles' doctrine and fellowship, in the breaking of bread, and in prayers. Then fear came upon every soul, and many wonders and signs were done through the apostles. Now all who believed were together, and had all things in common, and sold their possessions and goods, and divided them among all, as anyone had need.

> So continuing daily with one accord in the temple, and breaking bread from house to house, they ate their food with gladness and simplicity of heart, praising God and having favor with all the people. And the Lord added to the church daily those who were being saved.

Their emphasis was on teaching, relationships, worship, prayer, giving, and evangelism. In contrast with most churches today, they met daily, either in public or in homes, continually growing in strength and number. If the health of today's churches was measured against the first church that grew exponentially, very few would be considered healthy.

Hebrews 10:24-25 also encourages us with the words: "And let us consider one another in order to stir up love and good works, not forsaking the assembling of ourselves together, as is the manner of some, but exhorting one another, and so much the more as you see the Day approaching." This "Day" refers to the rapture, the time when Jesus will take the church to be with Him in the Father's house. As the rapture nears, these words encourage us to be more committed to the church, not less.

Further, Jesus taught, "I will build My church, and the gates of

Hades shall not prevail against it" (Matthew 16:18). Nothing can stop the people of God from doing the will of God as we await the kingdom of God. The phrase "I will build" has a continuative sense in the original Greek. He will build His true assembly of believers and keep on building it until the trumpet sounds and the archangel shouts.

Reason 6: Stand Firm in the Faith

In Ephesians 6, Paul speaks about wearing the armor of God, using the word translated "stand" three times. We are to:

- "Put on the whole armor of God, that you may be able to stand against the wiles of the devil" (v. 11).

- "Therefore take up the whole armor of God, that you may be able to withstand in the evil day, and having done all, to stand" (v. 13).

- "Stand therefore, having girded your waist with truth…" (v. 14).

James 5:7-8 also offers a wonderful word picture to remind us of the need to stand firm, patiently waiting for the Lord's coming: "Therefore be patient, brethren, until the coming of the Lord. See how the farmer waits for the precious fruit of the earth, waiting patiently for it until it receives the early and latter rain. You also be patient. Establish your hearts, for the coming of the Lord is at hand."

Another powerful example is found in the lives of the early apostles. The first time the apostles were arrested, Peter and John appeared at a trial where they were commanded to no longer speak in the name of Jesus. They responded, "Whether it is right in the sight of God to listen to you more than to God, you judge. For we cannot but speak the things which we have seen and heard" (Acts 4:19-20). Peter and John refused to back down from speaking what they had "seen and heard" about Jesus. Afterward, they prayed for even more boldness (Acts 4:23-31).

It is also interesting how the book of Revelation refers to the church. Its words are written to seven churches, about the church, for the church, predicting the triumphant return of the church. The church is His bride. When we speak about a person's wife, we seek to do so with respect. Why? A husband's wife is his most important relationship in this life. The bride of Christ is likewise a relationship of highest importance. How can we say we love Jesus yet hate His bride? Our faithful walk with the Lord must include a passion to remain connected with His bride, the church.

While it is true that an individual believer can know the salvation of the Lord, it is important to notice there are no isolated Christians in the book of Acts. Believers in Christ immediately banded together in local churches to serve the Lord in fellowship with one another (Acts 2:42; 1 Corinthians 1:9; Galatians 2:9; 1 John 1:3).

Reason 7: Avoid False Teaching

Jesus often warned His followers about the false teachers who would come. In Matthew 7:15, we read, "Beware of false prophets, who come to you in sheep's clothing, but inwardly they are ravenous wolves." These false prophets existed even in the time of Jesus. Their "sheep's clothing" referred to an exterior of peace and safety. However, the false teacher's true nature is to take and destroy what is good. Many false teachers sought to destroy Jesus during His ministry. Some continue to do so today.

Jesus predicts in Matthew 24:11, "Then many false prophets will rise up and deceive many." Matthew 24:24 (also Mark 13:22) adds, "For false christs and false prophets will rise and show great signs and wonders to deceive, if possible, even the elect." In the last days, false teachers will not be new, but they will be more numerous. Further, false teachers will become more convincing. The idea of deceiving "if possible, even the elect," does not refer to believers who will lose their salvation. Instead, it indicates these false teachings will be so well-developed and deceptive that even Christians could be easily misled.

This is precisely what we find now in our culture. Entire denominations that once based their ministry on the teachings of God's Word now accept seemingly every view under the sun. While continuing to cling to a form of godliness, they are no longer any different from the world (2 Timothy 3:5). Second Peter 2:1 warns, "But there were also false prophets among the people, even as there will be false teachers among you, who will secretly bring in destructive heresies, even denying the Lord who bought them, and bring on themselves swift destruction."

People walking away from Christianity should not surprise us. We can observe at least three reasons.[10] First, as the Western world becomes increasingly secular, it has become less popular in mainstream society to be viewed as a Christian. Thus, those that are looking to make a name for themselves in the world are no longer going to see being a Christian as socially acceptable but in fact detrimental to their goals.

Second, the Western educational system has radically turned against Christianity and turned toward secular humanism. This makes it much more difficult and confusing for young people to understand and believe their faith when they are constantly being bombarded with these ideas from trusted voices that have access to them for much of the week.

Finally, apostasy is not a new idea, but is present even in the pages of the New Testament. Judas himself traveled with Jesus for years and yet walked away from Him when it no longer suited his personal interests. Demas, in 2 Timothy 4, who was a traveler with Paul for years, walked away from his faith because he "loved this present world." In 2 Thessalonians 2, Paul even describes a time of great apostasy that will occur in the end times. However, there are many examples in the Bible of individuals who ran away from God for a time and returned to Him, such as John Mark and Jonah. God is always willing to forgive those who run away from Him and later return.

First John 4:1 adds, "Beloved, do not believe every spirit, but test the spirits, whether they are of God; because many false prophets have gone out into the world." We should not accept every teaching that claims to be from God, but must evaluate the teachings of any person or group with the standard of God's Word. Only then will we be able to avoid the false teachings that the Bible says will increase in number and intensity in the last days. As I have noted elsewhere:

The New Testament is clear in its warning about the dangers of apostasy in every generation but especially in the last days before the rapture of the church. The apostles urge us to stand true to the faith until Jesus comes to call us home to be with Him. Minor deviations of doctrine or personal preferences are not primary concerns. Apostasy involves the deliberate abandonment and repudiation of Jesus Christ and the Christian faith.[11]

Reason 8: Pray Fervently

An eighth reason God's Word provides is to pray fervently. Colossians 4:2-4 teaches, "Continue earnestly in prayer, being vigilant in it with thanksgiving; meanwhile praying also for us, that God would open to us a door for the word, to speak the mystery of Christ, for which I am also in chains, that I may make it manifest, as I ought to speak."

Our prayers are to be:

- intense: fervent and passionate
- ongoing: regular and continual
- thankful: filled with thanksgiving
- personal: from the heart
- intercessory: interceding for others
- asking for open doors for ministry
- desiring the salvation of the lost

Another way our amazing future should change our prayers is through increasing our boldness. Second Corinthians 3:12 says, "Therefore, since we have such hope, we use great boldness of speech." We know the Lord is coming soon. This should increase the way we ask God to intervene for the salvation of the lost, the purity of the church, and in meeting those in need. A believer who studies the end times is a believer who prays much of the time. Critics have claimed those who are heavenly minded are often no earthly good. In reality those who are heavenly minded have often done the most earthly good in light of their eternal destiny. By contrast, those who are earthly minded have done little.

While much more could be noted regarding prayer, two aspects to mention are *private* prayer and *public* prayer. Both are important! Regarding private prayer, Jesus taught, "But you, when you pray, go into your room, and when you have shut your door, pray to your Father who is in the secret place; and your Father who sees in secret will reward you openly" (Matthew 6:6). While some take this literally and even pray in a special room or location, the emphasis is on prayer focused on God apart from any public notice. God sees our prayers and answers according to His perfect will. Jesus was warning prideful people not to make a public spectacle of prayer just to call attention to themselves. Praying in secret is to be done in faith, believing that the God who sees in secret will reward you openly.

In addition, we are called to pray together. Matthew 18:20 says, "For where two or three are gathered together in My name, I am there in the midst of them." Our prayer gatherings do not need to be large to be effective. Yet there is something special about praying with other believers that is unique from praying alone. If the prayer of a righteous person is powerful and effective (James 5:16), then the prayers of many righteous people joined together certainly make an impact in seeking God's will on behalf of individuals, churches, and the world. The early Christians often gathered together for prayer, especially in times of persecution (Acts 12:12).

Reason 9: Encourage Other Believers

One of the foundational concepts of this book is that, for believers, prophecy should be encouraging because prophecy is good news. After describing the rapture in 1 Thessalonians 4, Paul says, "Therefore comfort one another with these words" (v. 18). Why should our understanding of the end times lead to encouragement?

- We have Jesus coming for us in the rapture (1 Thessalonians 4:13-17).

- We have heaven in our near future (John 14:1-3).
- We will receive eternal rewards (2 Corinthians 5:10).
- We will escape the coming tribulation (1 Thessalonians 5:9).
- We will return when Jesus defeats His enemies (Revelation 19:14).
- We will reign with Him for a thousand years in His kingdom (Revelation 20:4).
- We will dwell with the Lord for eternity in a new heaven and earth (Revelation 21–22).

How can we *not* be excited to encourage one another? We need not fear the "doom and gloom" of our culture or even the scary messages often communicated in discussions concerning the end times. Our future will be amazing! A loving Savior has provided everything we will ever need for time and eternity.

In addition, at the beginning of Paul's description of the rapture he says, "But I do not want you to be ignorant, brethren, concerning those who have fallen asleep, lest you sorrow as others who have no hope" (1 Thessalonians 4:13). At a funeral, there is understandably much sadness. Yet for those who die in the Lord, we can have sorrow and hope. Why? Because we know the one who has passed now rejoices in the presence of the Lord. Further, we will be reunited again one day with our believing loved ones who have passed on to heaven before us. We can rejoice even during times of much pain. "The sufferings of this present time are not worthy to be compared with the glory which shall be revealed in us" (Romans 8:18).

I love the words of 1 Corinthians 2:9:

> Eye has not seen, nor ear heard,
> Nor have entered into the heart of man
> The things which God has prepared for those who love
> Him.

Even the apostle John's visions in Revelation do not cover every blessing God has in store for our future. We have much to anticipate that we can use to encourage ourselves and others today—and every day—until Christ appears.

Reason 10: Occupy Until Jesus Returns

In the parable of the minas in Luke 19:11-27, Jesus "spoke another parable, because He was near Jerusalem and because they thought the kingdom of God would appear immediately" (v. 11). In the story, a leader called ten of his servants and gave each of them ten minas. (A mina was an amount of money worth about four months' wages for a worker in the first century. Take whatever you consider an average monthly income times four and you have an amount approximate to the level discussed in this parable.)

In the King James Version, the master "called his ten servants, and delivered them ten pounds, and said unto them, Occupy till I come." What does it mean to "occupy"? This was an Old English term that referred to doing business or working wisely. It did not mean occupy a seat and do nothing. The Greek term is *pragmateuomai*, which means to "carry on business," from which we get the English word *pragmatic*.[12] The servants were to invest the money they had received to benefit the leader upon his return. The obvious implication of this parable is that believers should be busy about the master's work in view of his certain return.

When the master returned, those who had invested wisely were told, "Well done, good servant" (v. 17). They were rewarded with authority over entire cities. In contrast, the servant who did nothing received judgment. This picture of reward for those who "occupy" until Jesus returns remains convicting today. We dare not take the investment of life, gifts, and opportunities God has given to us and bury them in the ground. We are to remain faithful and fruitful to His calling in our lives until He comes to us at the rapture or we go to Him at death. I appreciate how my friend Mark Hitchcock portrays the future as our final exam:

> The final exam is coming. If you know the Lord, you'll be there, and so will I. We can't call in sick. We don't get

to repeat the exam. There's no second chance. There's no makeup test. There's no grading on the curve. You get only one shot.

Now is your opportunity to prepare and get ready. You have the questions. Start studying now. Don't wait until the last minute to cram for the test. You and I have no excuse to fail. Let's commit to do all we can every day to ace the test, to get and *A* so we can hear those words, "well done, My good and faithful servant."[13]

Yet in this final exam, we need not fear the final outcome. As followers of Christ, we know the Creator of the test. He has personally provided everything necessary for us to succeed. Instead, we are called to live fully for God, anticipating our glorious future with Him for all eternity.

In his classic work, *The Saints' Everlasting Rest*, Richard Baxter said the hope of heaven is "the life and sum of all gospel promises and Christian privileges."[14] May it be true of you and me and motivate us to do something with our lives that will outlive us for all eternity!

A FINAL WORD:
WHAT ABOUT YOU?

In *The Popular Handbook on the Rapture*, I asked the question, "Is there any hope for our generation?"[1] I noted that throughout history, God has often moved to bless His people in a fresh and powerful way. Genuine spiritual awakening takes place as God's people are convicted of sin, repent, and gain new zeal and devotion for the Lord. In revival, the selfish indifference that so often dominates our lives is swept aside by a new and genuine desire to live for God.

Awakening renews our values and redirects our lives. It calls us to a more serious walk with Christ and results in substantial and abiding fruit (John 15:16; Galatians 5:22-23). The changes that occur, both in individual believers and in the church, speak convincingly to the world about what it really means to belong to Christ. Such revival comes when God's people pray, God's truth is proclaimed, and God's Spirit moves in our lives.

Until then, we can live with our eyes on the skies, watching for Christ to come, and with our feet on earth, working for Him until He comes. The balance of our expectation—that Jesus could return any moment—and our participation—serving faithfully until He comes— is what the Christian life is all about. Living in light of His coming keeps us focused on what matters most. It also keeps our attention on the balance between our present responsibilities and our future expectations.

The hope of the second coming is a powerful incentive to live right until Jesus comes. The ultimate encouragement toward right living is the fact that we will face our Lord when He returns. Each of us must be ready for that day to come so that we will hear Him say, "Well done, good and faithful servant." The apostle John said, "Continue in him, so that when he appears we may be confident and unashamed before him at his coming...All who have this hope in him purifies himself, just as he is pure" (1 John 2:28; 3:3 NIV).

Living as a faithful servant of the Lord, however, starts with making certain we have eternal life. The Bible reveals we can know we have eternal life. With absolute certainty, we can know Jesus died on the cross, rose from the dead, and is coming again. Going to heaven is not a matter of guesswork. It is not a matter of hope: "I hope I'm going to make it. I think I've done the right thing." No, Jesus did the right thing when He went to the cross and died in our place. He took the wrath of God against us on Himself when He rose from the dead to give us the gift of eternal life. We must put our faith and trust in what He did. The Bible tells us the truth that whoever will call on the name of the Lord will be saved (Romans 10:13).

There are many things that demand our attention in life. There are many voices calling to us, but none is greater than the voice of God. As time marches on, one thing is certain—we will face death at some point. Death is the great equalizer. It makes no difference who we are, when we face death we are facing an impartial judge. The Bible reminds that "all have sinned" (Romans 3:23) and the "wages of sin is death" (Romans 6:23). When death comes knocking at our door, all that really matters is that we are ready to face it.

You can know you are ready to meet the Lord because you have made the decision to put your faith and trust in Him. If you want to make that decision today, I encourage you to call on Him right now. You might want to pray something like this sincerely from your heart:

Almighty God, I am a sinner, and I know I need Your forgive-ness. I repent of my sins, believing Jesus died in my place, that He rose again, and that He is coming again. I want to know

for sure that He is coming for me. Today, I am committing my
heart, my life, and my soul to Him as my personal Savior. By
faith I want to receive the gift of eternal life from You forever.

Pray this in Jesus' name. Pray it with the confidence of an "amen." God will hear you and God will answer.

If you are making that decision for the very first time today, please write or go online and let me know of your decision. I would like to send you some material that will help you as you begin your new walk with Christ.

Email me at https://www.thekingiscoming.com.

Write to:

World Prophetic Ministry

PO Box 150439

Grand Rapids, MI 49515

Appendix

ESCAPING THE TRIBULATION: WHAT HAPPENS TO THOSE LEFT BEHIND?[1]

Jesus warned His disciples that in the last days there would be a period of time more horrific and traumatic than any other time in human history. He was, of course, referring to the great tribulation: "There will be great tribulation, such as has not been since the beginning of the world until this time, no, nor ever shall be" (Matthew 24:21).

The disciples were familiar with this prophesied time of anguish, for many of the Hebrew prophets of old had warned Israel about a future period of intense suffering. The prophet Jeremiah called it "the time of Jacob's trouble" (Jeremiah 30:7). Throughout the Old and New Testaments, the tribulation is referred to by a variety of names including "the day of the Lord" (1 Thessalonians 5:2), the seventieth week of Daniel (Daniel 9:27), "a day of devastation and desolation" (Zephaniah 1:15), "the wrath to come" (1 Thessalonians 1:10), "the hour of judgment" (Revelation 14:7), and "the great tribulation" (Matthew 24:21). Not only is the tribulation mentioned in more than sixty passages in the Bible, but more space is allotted to it than to any other subject except for salvation and the second coming of Christ.

Both the prophet Daniel and the apostle John stated this period would last seven years (Daniel 9:24-27; Revelation 11:1-3). After rising to power, the evil "prince who is to come" (Daniel 9:26), the Antichrist, will make a covenant with Israel. This event will signal the beginning of the seven-year tribulation period. Three and a half years into the tribulation, at the halfway point, the Antichrist will break the covenant by desecrating the rebuilt temple in Jerusalem. This will usher in the great tribulation, a period of suffering and terror worse than any that mankind has ever experienced. Although the tribulation lasts only seven years, the devastations unleashed during that time will seem endless to those who must face them.

The Nature of the Tribulation

Through various prophetic passages found in the Bible, we learn that the tribulation will be:

- a time of judgment for those who reject the Savior (2 Thessalonians 2:7-12)

- a time of devastation for those who rebel against God (Revelation 16–18)

- a time of decision for those who will be forced to choose between Christ and the Antichrist (Revelation 13:1-18; 14:9-11)

- a time of chaos designed to shake mankind's false sense of security (Revelation 15)

- a time of unprecedented revival, resulting in the greatest soul harvest in history (Revelation 7)

When will the tribulation take place? Although no exact date is given, the Bible indicates in Matthew 24:29-31 that it must occur immediately *before* the glorious appearing of Christ, when Jesus Himself returns to earth to destroy the Antichrist. It will also occur *after* the rapture of the church, when all those who have placed their trust in Jesus Christ will be instantly removed from the planet in order to meet the Lord in the air (1 Thessalonians 4:15-18).

Those who view the tribulation as primarily a time of wrath overlook the fact that it is also a time of mercy and grace. The Lord is not some angry monster heaping catastrophes upon the heads of innocent men and women. In reality, the people who suffer the judgments of God during the tribulation are not innocent. Not only do these rebels reject God and His free offer of salvation, they indulge in every vile sin known to mankind, including the massacre of those who come to Christ during this time. Even then, God appeals to these rebels to turn to Him through human witnesses (Revelation 11:3-6) and angelic messengers (Revelation 14:6-11). The tribulation judgments therefore serve a dual purpose: to punish hardened sinners and to move others to repentance. Joel 2:30-32 exemplifies this truth:

> I will show wonders in the heavens and in the earth:
> Blood and fire and pillars of smoke.
> The sun shall be turned into darkness,
> And the moon into blood,
> Before the coming of the great and awesome day of the
>   LORD.
> And it shall come to pass
> That whoever calls on the name of the LORD
> Shall be saved.

The Tribulation Saints

The untold millions who miss the rapture because of their rejection of God will still have an opportunity to become saved. The apostle John writes, "After these things I looked, and behold, a great multitude which no one could number, of all nations, tribes, peoples, and tongues, standing before the throne and before the Lamb, clothed with white robes, with palm branches in their hands" (Revelation 7:9).

These tribulation saints, whose numbers are so large they can't be counted, come to the Lord as a result of the tribulation's trials—

demonstrating that our holy God is a God who will continue to show His love and mercy to mankind even in the last days. When John wondered who these people are, the reply was, "These are the ones who come out of the great tribulation" (Revelation 7:14). No wonder the apostle Peter was able to write, "The Lord is not slack concerning His promise, as some count slackness, but is longsuffering toward us, not willing that any should perish but that all should come to repentance" (2 Peter 3:9).

Those Left Behind

In many respects, the rapture will set the stage for the coming tribulation. Following the disappearance of millions upon millions of Christians from the face of the earth, the world will be in a state of shock and chaos that defies comprehension. The recent coronavirus global pandemic was just a small glimpse of the worldwide chaos and confusion that will follow the rapture. This will prepare the way perfectly for the rise of the Antichrist. He will come to power peaceably using diplomacy—as represented by the rider on the white horse, the first of the four horsemen of the Apocalypse (Revelation 6:1-2). His charm and outward compassion will bring badly needed comfort to a populace on the brink of mass hysteria. But his global political, social, and economic control will lock the planet under his deceptive sway (2 Thessalonians 2:9-10).

The controlled media will be used to effectively coerce the world into adopting this new leader as the man of the hour. Ongoing efforts to discredit the Bible and other prophetic books that foretold the rapture and the rise of the Antichrist will be a top priority of the new world government. Every attempt will be made to convince the confused populace that those who have been left behind are, in fact, the lucky ones, even though nothing could be further from the truth.

The spiritual vacuum left by the disappearance of millions of Christians will also enable the Antichrist to further his plan for a forced one-world religion. This false religion will unite all religions—with the lone exception of biblical Christianity—into one. In the midst of all this, the Holy Spirit will work through the 144,000 evangelists and the two witnesses in Jerusalem to draw countless numbers of people to Christ during the tribulation—despite the fact that such a choice will most likely result in martyrdom.

The 144,000 Witnesses

The seventh seal introduces the seven trumpet judgments, which is why many prophecy students consider these judgments to be chronological: The first six seals presumably cover twenty-one months, then the breaking of the seventh seal introduces the next seven trumpet judgments, which take place during the second quarter or the second twenty-one months of the first half of the tribulation. The sealing of the 144,000 "servants of our God" probably occurs at the beginning of this period, and they witness all during it, along with the special two witnesses described in Revelation 11.

The Two Witnesses

In the last days, God will have the gospel message proclaimed worldwide so that people are without excuse about making a decision for Christ. During the first half of the tribulation, God not only uses the 144,000 Israelites from each of the twelve tribes who reach "a great multitude which no one could number" (Revelation 7:9), but He also establishes in and around Jerusalem two special witnesses endowed with supernatural powers (Revelation 11:3-6). Like Moses and Elijah, the two Old Testament witnesses who appeared with Jesus at His transfiguration (Matthew 17:1-8), they will be able to bring a series of plagues and call down fire from above (Revelation 11:5-6).

During the tribulation, two powerful opposing forces will be at work: 1) the 144,000 servants of God who bring forth a mighty soul harvest, and 2) those who refuse to repent from their enormous sinfulness. It will be the same as in our day right now, with the church witnessing for the Lord on the one hand, and others rejecting the Savior on the other, except that the opposition will be intensified during the tribulation period.

Also, because the civil government described in Revelation 13 will be under the total control of the Antichrist and his evil forces, Christians will be persecuted and martyred in large numbers. Many people will become saved through the soul harvest, but for a while, it will seem as if Christians are on the losing end of the battle because the Antichrist will be in control of the world. However, we know that ultimately, Christ—and His people—will be the victor.

World War III

After his peaceful ascension to power, the Antichrist will initiate what we might call World War III (Revelation 6:3-4) against the regional leaders who will be in power during this time. Death and destruction will be brought to this earth on a massive scale never before known. This battle may involve a nuclear exchange and will be followed by widespread inflation, famine, and disease. Possibly due in part to nuclear fallout, plagues will sweep across the land and death will come to a fourth of the world's population (Revelation 6:5-8). All the while, the Antichrist will be carrying out his vengeance against those who have chosen to follow Christ instead of him (Revelation 6:9-11). And the killing of millions of tribulation saints will escalate as the world sinks further into death and despair.

Up to this point, the judgments that have come upon earth during the tribulation are largely the result of man's actions. Armies are marching, men are fighting, and the world is at war. From here onward, however, the judgments will be acts of divine retribution. Revelation 6:12-15 describes a massive earthquake so large that "every mountain and island was moved out of its place" (verse 14).

Apparently, there will be a series of massive volcanic eruptions as well, which will cause the sky to darken and the moon to appear red. The apostle John also writes of meteor-like objects that come crashing down onto the earth. So incredible are these events that earth's inhabitants will realize they are witnessing God's judgments right before their eyes: "The kings of the earth, the great men, the rich men, the commanders, the mighty men, every slave and every free man, hid themselves in the caves and in the rocks of the mountains, and said to the mountains and rocks, 'Fall on us and hide us from the face of Him who sits on the throne and from the wrath of the Lamb! For the great day of His wrath has come, and who is able to stand?'" (Revelation 6:15-17).

Then hail, fire, and blood will rain down from the sky, causing a third of the earth's trees and grass to burn up. Two more meteors will fall from the sky and kill a third of the sea life, destroy a third of the ships at sea, and poison a third of the earth's fresh water supply. Darkness will continue to envelope the land as the light from the sun and moon is dimmed by a third.

Hell on Earth

Revelation chapter 9 describes a plague of locustlike creatures that descend upon the earth and have the ability to sting people. For five months, these creatures will torment but not kill unbelievers:

> Out of the smoke locusts came upon the earth. And to them was given power, as the scorpions of the earth have power. They were commanded not to harm the grass of the earth, or any green thing, or any tree, but only those men who do not have the seal of God on their foreheads. And they were not given authority to kill them, but to torment them for five months. Their torment was like the torment of a scorpion when it strikes a man. In those days men will seek death and will not find it; they will desire to die, and death will flee from them (Revelation 9:3-6).

If that weren't enough, armies of demonic horsemen will then be unleashed and kill another third of the world's population (Revelation 9:13-19).

The Mark of the Beast

As mentioned previously, halfway into the tribulation, the Antichrist will break his treaty with the nation of Israel, desecrate the rebuilt temple in Jerusalem, and kill the two witnesses who have been proclaiming the gospel (Revelation 11:3-12). He will then seize total control over the monetary system of the world (Revelation 13:16-18), requiring all to carry his mark, which in some way will consist of the number 666. This is the prophesied mark of the beast, and without it, no one will be able to buy or sell: "He causes all, both small and great, rich and poor, free and slave, to receive a mark on their right hand or on their foreheads, and that no one may buy or sell except one who has the mark" (Revelation 13:16-17).

Even a few short years ago, such a prospect would have seemed inconceivable. But now, with computerized electronic financial transactions occurring worldwide, the ability to control and track the purchases of every human being is not only possible but inevitable. Every global economic crisis pushes us closer to this reality every day that passes. It is only a matter of time until a global dictator will control the global economy on which we are all dependent.

Preparing for Armageddon

Meanwhile, as the tribulation progresses, the judgments of God will continue to afflict the ungodly. Loathsome sores will break out upon those who have the mark of the beast. The sea and remaining fresh water will be turned into blood. Heat from the sun will scorch the unrepentant, and darkness will envelope the kingdom of the Antichrist (Revelation 16:1-11).

Then the Euphrates River will dry up, allowing the armies of the east to march unhindered to Israel to begin the battle of Armageddon.

The bloodshed will reach unparalleled proportions. A tremendous earthquake will level the cities of the world, and hailstones weighing as much as a hundred pounds will fall to the earth. Unfortunately, many of the ungodly still will not repent, despite the severity of these judgments:

> There was a great earthquake, such a mighty and great earthquake as had not occurred since men were on the earth. Now the great city was divided into three parts, and the cities of the nations fell. And great Babylon was remembered before God, to give her the cup of the wine of the

fierceness of His wrath. Then every island fled away, and the mountains were not found. And great hail from heaven fell upon men, each hailstone about the weight of a talent. Men blasphemed God because of the plague of the hail, since that plague was exceedingly great (Revelation 16:18-21).

And with that, the judgments will draw to an end. The glorious appearing of Christ comes next. He will be in the air accompanied by the armies of heaven, which consist of all those who were raptured to heaven (Revelation 19:11-14). Christ will then descend to earth in power and glory to win the battle of Armageddon. He will cast the beast (Antichrist) and false prophet into the lake of fire and bind Satan in the abyss for a thousand years. Then He will initiate His millennial reign on earth (Revelation 19:19–20:3).

Understanding the Judgments of Revelation

The book of Revelation includes three sets of judgments (seven seals, seven trumpets, and seven bowls)—twenty-one total judgments that will unfold during the seven-year tribulation period. An overview of these judgments provides a helpful understanding of how these events will unfold.

Seal Judgments (Revelation 6)

- Seal One: The rider on the white horse (6:1-2)
- Seal Two: The rider on the red horse (6:3-4)
- Seal Three: The rider on the black horse (6:5-6)
- Seal Four: The rider on the pale horse (6:7-8)
- Seal Five: The martyred tribulation saints (6:9-11)
- Seal Six: A great earthquake (6:12-17)
- Seal Seven: Silence in heaven—beginning of trumpet judgments (8:1-6)

Trumpet Judgments (Revelation 8–9)

- Trumpet One: One-third of vegetation destroyed (8:7)
- Trumpet Two: One-third of the sea turned into blood (8:8-9)
- Trumpet Three: One-third of the waters contaminated (8:10-11)
- Trumpet Four: One-third of the sky darkened (8:12)
- Trumpet Five: The "first woe": locustlike creatures plague the earth (9:1-12)
- Trumpet Six: The "second woe": army of 200,000,000 men from the east destroys one-third of all people (9:13-19)
- Trumpet Seven: The "third woe": beginning of the seven bowl judgments (11:15-19)

Bowl Judgments (Revelation 16)

- Bowl One: Terrible sores on those who follow the Antichrist (16:2)
- Bowl Two: All the seas turned into blood (16:3)
- Bowl Three: All fresh water turned to blood (16:4-7)
- Bowl Four: Terrible heat upon the earth (16:8-9)
- Bowl Five: Supernatural darkness on the earth (16:10-11)
- Bowl Six: Euphrates River dries up and an army marches toward Armageddon (16:12-16)
- Bowl Seven: Massive moving of the earth's crust and hundred-pound hailstones (16:17-21)

What Begins the Tribulation?

The prophecy of Daniel 9:27 tells us exactly what will start the tribulation: when "he [the prince who is to come] shall confirm a covenant with many for one week." It seems that the Antichrist will make a covenant with the nation of Israel to ensure their protection. However, he will break this covenant after three-and-a-half years. This does not mean that the treaty itself will be a seven-year treaty, as opposed to one of indefinite length, but that it will be broken in the middle of the seventieth "week" (seven) of Daniel 9:27. Since the seventieth "seven" refers to the seven years of the tribulation period, the reader understands that the treaty will be broken at the halfway point.

Daniel's prophecy may relate to the rider on the white horse of Revelation 6, who comes in peace. It appears the Antichrist will offer peace to the world and make a covenant with Israel, bringing peace to the Jewish people, who will then be able to rebuild their temple and presumably reinstate their sacrifices again—for three-and-a-half years! However, this rider carries a bow and is bent on conquest (Revelation 6:2).

Daniel 9:27 continues:

> But in the middle of the week [of years]
> He shall bring an end to sacrifice and offering.
> And on the wing of abominations shall be one who
> makes desolate.

The Antichrist will break his covenant with the Jews in the middle of the tribulation (which agrees with Revelation 11 and 13) and will launch the greatest time of desolation in the history of the world. How long will it last? "Until the consummation, which is determined" (9:27). This is the same as "the time of the end," meaning the end of the seventy "sevens" (*heptads*) or 490 years of God's dealing with the Jews.

In summary, then, the tribulation will begin when the covenant of peace is confirmed between the coming new world government (headed by the Antichrist) and the nation of Israel. But halfway through the seven years, the Antichrist will break that covenant and begin to persecute the nation of Israel, and they will become "desolate."

Many Christians think the rapture of the church begins the tribulation, but while it's possible the rapture and the signing of the covenant may take place very close together, the Bible is not specific on that subject. Still, there has never been a world ruler who has made a covenant of peace with Israel and then broken that covenant after three-and-a-half years. This obviously means that the fulfillment of these events is still in the future.

The timing of the last days is in God's hands. From a human standpoint, we appear to be standing on the threshold of the last days. The pieces of the puzzle are all in place. As the sands of time slip through the hourglass of history, we are all moving closer to an appointment with destiny. The only question is, How much time is left?

Israel is back in the land. The Middle East is in constant turmoil. The global economy already exists. Global pandemics threaten the planet. Weapons of mass destruction have already been invented. What else must God do to get our attention? The stage is already set for the last days.

Every generation of Christians has lived with the hope of the imminent return of Christ. We believe that He could come at any moment. There is no prophetic event that must be fulfilled before He could return. In fact, certain events indicate that we are closer to the end than ever before.

So, what are you waiting for? The clock is ticking, and your time may be running out. The time to come to Christ for salvation is right now! The Bible says,

> "Today, if you will hear His voice,
> Do not harden your hearts."
>
> (Hebrews 4:7)

Instead, "Let us therefore come boldly to the throne of grace, that we may obtain mercy and find grace to help in time of need" (4:16). His grace is available right now. All you have to do is receive it by faith, and God's eternal plan for your future will begin the moment you believe.

NOTES

Preface

1. Joe Stowell, *Eternity* (Chicago: Moody Press, 1995), 13.

1. Does God Really Have a Future for Me?

1. Ron Rhodes, *The Wonder of Heaven* (Eugene, OR: Harvest House Publishers, 2009), 95.

2. Greg Laurie, "A Good and Faithful Servant," *Harvest Ministries*, September 6, 2007. Accessed at https://harvest.org/resources/devotion/a-good-and-faithful-servant/.

3. Arnold G. Fruchtenbaum, *The Footsteps of Messiah*, rev. ed. (Tustin, CA: Ariel Ministries, 2003), 352.

4. Adapted from Tony Garland, *A Commentary on the Book of Revelation*, Bible Gateway. Accessed at https://www.biblestudytools.com/commentaries/revelation/revelation-20/revelation-20-2.html.

5. Ron Rhodes, *The Wonder of Heaven* (Eugene, OR: Harvest House Publishers, 2009), 12.

6. Norman Geisler, *Systematic Theology: In One Volume* (Grand Rapids, MI: Bethany House, 2011), electronic edition.

2. The Rapture

1. Gerald Stanton, *Kept from the Hour* (Haysville, NC: Schoettle, 1991), 108.

2. Robert H. Gundry, *The Church and the Tribulation* (Grand Rapids, MI: Zondervan, 1973), 29.

3. John A. Sproule, *In Defense of Pretribulationism* (Winona Lake, IN: BMH Books, 1980), 12.

4. William Mounce, ed *Mounce's Complete Expository Dictionary of Old and New Testament Words* (Grand Rapids, MI: Zondervan, 2006), 666.

5. For a complete list of "raptures" (Greek, *harpazo*), see Ed Hindson and Mark Hitchcock, *Can We Still Believe in the Rapture?* (Eugene, OR: Harvest House Publishers, 2017), 46-62. Even Jesus' ascension is described by the term *harpazo* (Revelation 12:5). The raptured church is pictured by the gold-crowned, white-robed elders in heaven (Revelation 4:4). Cf. David Hocking and Tim Demy, "Elders (24)" in Ed Hindson, Mark Hitchcock, and Tim LaHaye, eds., *The Harvest Handbook of Bible Prophecy* (Eugene, OR: Harvest House Publishers, 2020), 105-7.

6. Paul Benware, *Understanding the End Times* (Chicago: Moody Press, 1995), 181.

7. Millard J. Erickson, *Introducing Christian Doctrine* (Grand Rapids, MI: Baker Academic, 2015), electronic edition.

8. Ron Rhodes, *The End Times in Chronological Order* (Eugene, OR: Harvest House, 2012), 48.

9. Thomas D. Ice, "Why I Believe the Bible Teaches Rapture Before Tribulation," *Digital Commons@ Liberty University*, May 2009. Accessed at https://digitalcommons.liberty.edu/cgi/viewcontent.cgi?article=1117&context=pretrib_arch.

10. Stanton, *Kept from the Hour,* 50.

11. J. Dwight Pentecost, *Things to Come: A Study in Biblical Eschatology* (Grand Rapids, MI: Zondervan Academic, 2010), 216.

12. Tim LaHaye, *Revelation Unveiled* (Grand Rapids, MI: Zondervan, 1999), 100.

13. Renald Showers, *Maranatha: Our Lord Come!* (Bellmawr, NJ: Friends of Israel, 1995), 214.

14. Thomas Ice, "The Meaning of 'Earth Dwellers' and the Book of Revelation," *Pre-Trib Research Center*. Accessed at https://www.pre-trib.org/articles/all-articles/message/the-meaning-of-earth-dwellers-and-the-book-of-revelation/read.

15. *Our Daily Bread*, November 10, 1991. Accessed at https://www.ministry127.com/resources/illustration/work-until-jesus-comes.

3. The Father's House

1. David Jeremiah, *The Book of Signs* (Nashville, TN: Thomas Nelson, 2019), 182.

2. Thomas L. Constable, "Notes on John," *Sonic Light*. Accessed at https://www.planobiblechapel.org/tcon/notes/html/nt/john/john.htm.

3. D.A. Carson, *The Gospel According to John*, Pillar New Testament Commentary (Grand Rapids, MI: Wm. B. Eerdmans, 1991), electronic edition.

4. Arno C. Gaebelein, *The Gospel of John*, 4 vols., reprint ed. (Chicago: Moody Press, 1970), 268.

5. John MacArthur, "Heavenly Promises," February 15, 2015. Accessed at https://www.gty.org/library/sermons-library/43-72/heavenly-promises.

6. Kenneth Gangel, *John*, Holman New Testament Commentary (Nashville, TN: Broadman & Holman Publishers, 2000), electronic edition.

7. E.M. Bounds, *Heaven: A Place, A City, A Home* (Grand Rapids, MI: Baker, 1975), 7.

8. Jeremiah, *Book of Signs*, 188.

9. John MacArthur, "Heaven," in E. Hindson, et al., *The Harvest Handbook of Bible Prophecy* (Eugene, OR: Harvest House Publishers, 2020), 146-49.

10. Ibid., 146.

11. John MacArthur, *The Glory of Heaven* (Wheaton, IL: Crossway Books, 1996), 60.

12. Thomas Ice, "Heaven: Our Future Home," *Pre-Trib Research Center*. Accessed at https://www.pre-trib.org/articles/all-articles/message/heaven-our-future-home/read.

13. "Abraham's Bosom—What Is It?" *CompellingTruth.org*. Accessed at https://www.compellingtruth.org/Abrahams-bosom.html.

14. Ron Rhodes, *The Wonder of Heaven* (Eugene, OR: Harvest House Publishers), 55.

15. Billy Graham, "Answers," *Billy Graham Evangelistic Association*, August 22, 2017. Accessed at https://billygraham.org/answer/will-we-be-reunited-with-our-loved-ones-in-heaven.

16. Richard Baxter, as cited in John MacArthur, *The Glory of Heaven* (Wheaton, IL: Crossway, 1996), 172.

17. W.A. Criswell and Paige Patterson, *Heaven* (Carol Stream, IL: Tyndale House Publishers, 1991), 33.

18. Charles Ryrie, *Ryrie's Basic Theology* (Chicago: Moody Press, 1999), electronic edition.

19. John Hart, *50 Things You Need to Know About Heaven* (Minneapolis: Bethany House, 2014), 39.

20. Arthur W. Pink, *Exposition of the Gospel of John*, 3 vols. in 1, reprint ed. (Grand Rapids, MI: Zondervan Publishing House, 1973), 2:349-50.

21. Erwin Lutzer, *One Minute After You Die* (Chicago: Moody Publishers, 1997), 70.

22. Quoted by Bounds, *Heaven*, 140.

4. The Judgment Seat of Christ

1. Woodrow Kroll, *Facing Your Final Job Review* (Wheaton, IL: Crossway Books, 2008), 44.

2. Mark Hitchcock, *Heavenly Rewards* (Eugene, OR: Harvest House Publishers, 2019), 13.

3. J. Dwight Pentecost, *Things to Come: A Study in Biblical Eschatology* (Grand Rapids, MI: Zondervan Academic, 2010), 221.

4. Don Stewart, "What Is the Judgment Seat of Christ? (The Bema)," *Blue Letter Bible*. Accessed at https://www.blueletterbible.org/faq/don_stewart/don_stewart_144.cfm.

5. "The Doctrine of Rewards: The Judgment Seat (Bema) of Christ," *Bible.org*. Accessed at https://bible.org/article/doctrine-rewards-judgment-seat-bema-christ.

6. John MacArthur, *2 Corinthians*, MacArthur New Testament Commentary Series (Chicago: Moody, 2003), 176-77.

7. Mark Hitchcock, "An Overview of Pretribulational Arguments." Accessed at https://s3.amazonaws.com/dougriggs/Hitchcock-AnOverviewofPretribu.pdf.

8. J. Dwight Pentecost, *Things to Come: A Study in Biblical Eschatology* (Grand Rapids, MI: Zondervan, 1958), 221.

9. Lewis Sperry Chafer and John F. Walvoord, *Major Bible Themes* (Grand Rapids, MI: Zondervan Academic, 2010), 282.

10. Lehman Strauss, "The Future Judgment of the Believer," *Bible.org*. Accessed at https://bible.org/seriespage/future-judgment-believer.

11. Erwin Lutzer, *Your Eternal Reward: Triumph and Tears at the Judgment Seat of Christ* (Chicago: Moody Publishers, 2015), electronic edition.

12. Samuel L. Hoyt, "The Negative Aspects of the Christian's Judgment," *Bibliotheca Sacra* (April-June 1980): 131.

13. David Jeremiah, *The Book of Signs* (Nashville, TN: Thomas Nelson, 2019), 210-11.

14. Strauss, "Future Judgment of the Believer."

15. David Jeremiah, *Things That Matter: Living a Live of Purpose* (Nashville, TN: W Publishing Group, 2003), 62.

16. John Stott, *Romans: God's Good News for the World* (Downers Grove, IL: InterVarsity Press, 1994), 237.

17. Jonathan Falwell, *One Great Truth: Finding Your Answers to Life* (New York: Simon & Schuster, 2009), electronic edition.

18. Lutzer, *Your Eternal Reward*, electronic edition.

19. Adrian Rogers, "The Judgment Seat of Christ," June 30, 2014, *Love Worth Finding Ministries*. Accessed at www.lwf.org/bible-study/the-judgement-seat-of-christ.

5. The Marriage of the Lamb

1. Harold Wilmington, "Marriage of the Lamb," in Ed Hindson, March Hitchcock, Tim LaHaye, eds., *The Harvest Handbook of Bible Prophecy* (Eugene, OR: Harvest House, 2020), 229.

2. Charles C. Ryrie, *The Miracles of Our Lord* (Dubuque, IA: ECS Ministries, 2005), 15.

3. Jason Sobel, quoted in Kathie Lee Gifford, *The Rock, the Road and the Rabbi* (Nashville, TN: Thomas Nelson, 2018), 60.

4. Daniel Mitchell, *Second Corinthians: Grace Under Siege* (Chattanooga, TN: AMG Publishers, 2009), 33.

5. J. Dwight Pentecost, *Things to Come: A Study in Biblical Eschatology* (Grand Rapids, MI: Zondervan, 1958), 226.

6. Ibid., 228.

7. Ron Rhodes, *The End Times in Chronological Order* (Eugene, OR: Harvest House, 2012), 72.

8. Arnold Fruchtenbaum, *The Footsteps of the Messiah* (San Antonio, TX: Ariel Ministries, 2003), n.p.

9. Tim LaHaye, *Revelation Unveiled* (Grand Rapids, MI: Zondervan, 1999), 295.

10. John Walvoord, *The Church in Prophecy*, second edition (Grand Rapids, MI: Kregel, 1999), 144.

11. Mark Hitchcock, *The End* (Carol Stream, IL: Tyndale House Publishers, 2012), 225.

12. Walvoord, *Church in Prophecy*, 141.

13. Ray C. Stedman, *God's Final Word* (Grand Rapids, MI: Discovery House, 1991), electronic edition.

14. Pentecost, *Things to Come*), 227.

15. Tony Garland, "The Jewish Wedding Analogy," *BibleStudyTools.com*. Accessed at https://www .biblestudytools.com/commentaries/revelation/related-topics/the-jewish-wedding-analogy .html#98513.

16. Hitchcock, *The End*, 227.

17. "Are There Parallels Between Jewish Wedding Traditions and Our Relationship to Christ?" *Got Questions Ministries*. Accessed at https://www.gotquestions.org/Jewish-wedding-traditions .html.

18. Robert H. Mounce, *The Book of Revelation*, New International Commentary on the New Testament, vol. 27 (Grand Rapids, MI: Wm. B. Eerdmans Publishing, 1998), 347.

19. J. Hampton Keathley III, "The Second Coming of Christ (Rev 19:1-21)," *Bible.org*. Accessed at https://bible.org/seriespage/26-second-coming-christ-rev-191-21.

20. Garland, "Jewish Wedding Analogy."

21. Thomas Constable, "Revelation," *Sonic Light*. Accessed at https://www.planobiblechapel.org/ tcon/notes/html/nt/revelation/revelation.htm.

22. Renald E. Showers, "Behold, the Bridegroom Comes!" *The Berean Call*, April 1, 2011. Accessed at https://www.thebereancall.org/content/april-2011-extra-behold-the-bridegroom-comes.

23. Steve Herzig, "The Jewish Wedding," *Israel My Glory*, August/September 1993. Accessed at https://israelmyglory.org/article/the-jewish-wedding.

24. Renald E. Showers, "Jewish Marriage Customs." Accessed at http://www.biblestudymanuals .net/jewish_marriage_customs.htm.

25. Keathley, "Second Coming of Christ."

26. Renald E. Showers, *Maranatha: Our Lord Come* (Bellmawr, NJ: Friends of Israel Gospel Ministry, 1995), electronic edition.

6. The Triumphant Return

1. Adapted from my commentary *Revelation: Unlocking the Future* (Chattanooga, TN: AMG Publishers, 2002), 187-97.

2. René Pache, *The Return of Jesus Christ* (Chicago: Moody Press, 1955), 353.

3. David Jeremiah, *The Book of Signs* (Nashville, TN: Thomas Nelson, 2019), 352.

4. Anthony Hoekema, *The Bible and the Future* (Grand Rapids, MI: Wm. B. Eerdmans, 1979), 223-38. Hoekema goes to great lengths attempting to prove that the marriage in chapter 20 preceeds the return in chapter 19, which defies the clear logic of the sequence of events that are obvious in the text. Thus, he is forced to admit: "If, then, one thinks Revelation 20 as setting forth what follows chronologically after what has been described in chapter 19, one would indeed conclude that the millennium of Revelation 20:1-6 will come after the return of Christ" (226).

5. Robert Gromacki, "Where Is 'the Church' in Revelation 4–19?" in Thomas Ice and Timothy Demy, eds., *When the Trumpet Sounds* (Eugene, OR: Harvest House, 1995), 355.

6. G.R. Beasley-Murray, *The Book of Revelation* (London: Marshall Morgan & Scott, 1978), 270.

7. Ibid., 271.

8. Ibid., 273-274.

9. Bruce Metzger, *Breaking the Code: Understanding the Book of Revelation* (Nashville, TN: Abingdon Press, 1995), 90.

10. Ibid., 90.

11. Robert Thomas, *Revelation 8-22* (Chicago: Moody Press, 1995), 381.

12. Warren Wiersbe, *Wiersbe's Expository Outlines on the New Testament* (Wheaton, IL: Victor Books, 1992), electronic edition.

13. A.W. Boehm, "Preface" to Johann Arndt's *True Christianity* (London: Brown & Downing, 1720), xxii.

7. The Millennial Kingdom

1. J. Richard Middleton, *A New Heaven and A New Earth* (Grand Rapids, MI: Baker Academic, 2014), 24.

2. Glenn Kreider, "The Doctrine of the Future in Jonathan Edwards," in Jeffrey Bingham and Glenn Kreider, eds., *Eschatology* (Grand Rapids, MI: Kregel Academic, 2016), 356.

3. See Lorraine Boettner, *The Millennium* (Philadelphia: Presbyterian & Reformed, 1957); R.J. Rushdoony, *Thy Kingdom Come* (Fairfax, VA: Chalcedon, 1975); J.J. Davis, *Christ's Victorious Kingdom* (Grand Rapids, MI: Baker, 1986).

4. See G.C. Berkouwer, *The Return of Christ* (Grand Rapids, MI: Wm. B. Eerdmans, 1962); A. Hoekema, *The Bible and the Future* (Grand Rapids, MI: Wm. B. Eerdmans, 1979).

5. See J. Dwight Pentecost, *Things to Come* (Grand Rapids, MI: Zondervan, 1958); John Walvoord, *Major Bible Prophecies* (New York: Harper Collins, 1991); Mark Hitchcock, *The End* (Carol Stream, IL: Tyndale House, 2012).

6. See Alva McClain, *The Greatness of the Kingdom* (Chicago: Moody Press, 1959), 22-57.

7. Pentecost, *Things to Come*, 370.

8. Tim LaHaye, *Revelation Unveiled* (Grand Rapids, MI: Zondervan, 1999), 346.

9. John MacArthur, *Matthew 24-28*, MacArthur New Testament Commentary (Chicago: Moody Publishers, 1989), 104.

10. Charles Ryrie, *Ryrie's Basic Theology* (Chicago: Moody Press, 1999), electronic edition.

11. Charles Dyer, "Ezekiel," eds. John F. Walvoord and Roy B. Zuck in *Bible Knowledge Commentary* (Colorado Springs, CO: SP Publications, 1983), electronic edition.

12. Ron Rhodes, *The End Times in Chronological Order* (Eugene, OR: Harvest House, 2012), 192-93.

13. Lamar Cooper, *Ezekiel*, New American Commentary Series (Nashville, TN: Broadman & Holman Publishers, 1994), 381. Cf. also John Whitcomb, "Millennial Sacrifices," in Ed Hindson, Mark Hitchcock, Tim LaHaye, *Harvest Handbook of Bible Prophecy* (Eugene, OR: Harvest House Publishers, 2020), 248-51.

14. Merrill Unger, *Unger's Bible Handbook: An Essential Guide to Understanding the Bible* (Chicago: Moody Press, 1966), 380.

15. Rhodes, *End Times in Chronological Order*, 194.

16. Walvoord, "Revelation," in *Bible Knowledge Commentary*, electronic edition.

17. Mark Hitchcock, *The End* (Carol Stream, IL: Tyndale House, 2012), 421.

8. The New Heavens and New Earth

1. Randy Alcorn, *Heaven* (Carol Stream, IL: Tyndale House, 2004), 11.

2. Mark Hitchcock, *The End* (Carol Stream, IL: Tyndale House, 2012), 431.

3. Robert Jeffress, *A Place Called Heaven* (Grand Rapids, MI: Baker, 2017), 103.

4. W.A. Criswell, "The New Creation," *W.A. Criswell Sermon Library*, September 16,1984. Accessed at www.wacriswell.com/sermons/1984/the-new-creation1.

5. David Jeremiah, *The Book of Signs* (Nashville, TN: Thomas Nelson Publishing, 2019), 396.

6. William Hendriksen, *The Bible on the Life Hereafter* (Grand Rapids, MI: Baker, 1959), 206.

7. John Walvoord, *Major Bible Prophecies* (Grand Rapids, MI: Zondervan, 1991), 413-14.

8. John MacArthur, *The Glory of Heaven* (Wheaton, IL: Crossway Books, 1996), 61.

9. John F. Walvoord, "Revelation," eds. John F. Walvoord and Roy B. Zuck in *Bible Knowledge Commentary* (Colorado Springs, CO: SP Publications, 1983), electronic edition.

10. Bruce Metzger, *Breaking the Code: Understanding the Book of Revelation* (Nashville, TN: Abingdon Press, 1993), 98.

11. Bernard Ramm, *Them He Glorified* (Grand Rapids, MI: Eerdmans, 1963), 136.

12. Robert H. Mounce, *The Book of Revelation*, New International Commentary on the New Testament, vol. 27 (Grand Rapids, MI: Wm. B. Eerdmans Publishing, 1998), 391-92.

13. Jeremiah, *The Book of Signs*, 410.

14. Ibid., 402.

15. A.T. Pierson, as cited in Ron Rhodes, *The End Times in Chronological Order* (Eugene, OR: Harvest House, 2012), 222-23.

16. Alcorn, *Heaven*, 251.

17. Randall Price, "New Jerusalem," in *The Harvest Handbook of Bible Prophecy*, eds. Ed Hindson, Mark Hitchcock, Tim LaHaye (Eugene, OR: Harvest House Publishers, 2020), 271.

9. The Final Picture

1. Eric Lyons, "Revelation and the Old Testament," *Apologetics Press*. Accessed at http://apologeticspress.org/apcontent.aspx?category=11&article=886. See also Ranko Stefanovic, *Revelation of*

Jesus Christ: Commentary on the Book of Revelation, (Berrien Springs, MI: Andrews University Press, 2009), 18; Brooke Foss Westcott and Fenton John Anthony Hort, *The New Testament in the Original Greek* (London: Macmillan Publishers, 1911); H.B. Swete, *The Apocalypse of Saint John* (London: Macmillan Publishers, 1911, reprinted, Grand Rapids, MI: Wm. B. Eerdmans Publishing Co., n.d).

2. Opeyemi T. Oladosu and Caleb O. Alu, "The Use of the Old Testament in the Book of Revelation," *American Journal of Biblical Theology,* vol. 17, issue 8, February 28, 2016. Accessed at https://www.biblicaltheology.com/Research/OladosuT01.pdf.

3. I. Paige Patterson, *Revelation,* New American Commentary (Nashville, TN: B & H Publishing Group, 2012), electronic edition.

4. Thomas Constable, "Notes on Revelation," *Sonic Light.* Accessed at https://www.planobible chapel.org/tcon/notes/html/nt/revelation/revelation.htm.

5. Mark Hitchcock, *101 Answers to Questions About the Book of Revelation* (Eugene, OR: Harvest House Publishers, 2012), 241.

6. Warren W. Wiersbe, *Wiersbe's Expository Outlines on the New Testament* (Colorado Springs, CO: Victor Books, 1992), electronic edition.

7. As noted in Michael F. Foss, *Real Faith for Real Life: Living the Six Marks of Discipleship* (Minneapolis, MN: Augsburg Books, 2004), 61.

8. Quotations from "25 Quotes from Influential Christians about the Bible," *Crosswalk.com,* November 29, 2016. Accessed at https://www.crosswalk.com/faith/spiritual-life/inspiring -quotes/25-quotes-from-influential-christians-about-the-bible.html.

9. William T. Dobson, *History of the Bassandyne Bible, the First Printed in Scotland* (Edinburgh and London: W. Blackwood and Sons, 1887), 132. English updated. Also found in the introduction to the *MacArthur Study Bible.*

10. John F. Walvoord, *Revelation,* rev. and ed. Philip E. Rawley and Mark Hitchcock (Chicago: Moody Publishers, 2011), electronic edition.

11. Charles Spurgeon, "Till We Meet Again," *Spurgeon's Sermons,* No. 1628. Accessed at https://ccel .org/ccel/spurgeon/sermons27.liv.html?scrBook=Rev&scrCh=22&scrV=21#highlight.

10. Why Your Future Matters Today

1. Grant Jeffrey, *Heaven: Homeward Bound* (Colorado Springs, CO: Waterbrook Press, 1996), 243.

2. J.I. Packer, "Glory of God," in Sinclair Ferguson and David Wright, *New Dictionary of Theology* (Downers Grove, IL: InterVarsity Press, 1988), 272.

3. Francis Schaeffer, *The God Who Is There* (Chicago: InterVarsity Press, 1968), 152, 154.

4. John A. Witmer, "Romans," eds. John F. Walvoord and Roy B. Zuck in *Bible Knowledge Commentary* (Colorado Springs, CO: SP Publications, 1983), electronic edition.

5. "Scripture Access Statistics," *Wycliffe Global Alliance,* October 2019. Accessed at https://www .wycliffe.net/resources/scripture-access-statistics/.

6. "Latest Bible Translation Figures Show Progress," *Wycliffe Bible Translators,* October 1, 2019. Accessed at https://www.wycliffe.org.uk/resources/press-releases latest-bible-translation-figures/#.

7. From Faith Comes by Hearing, January 2020. Accessed at https://www.faithcomesbyhearing .com/mission/strategy.

8. David E. Garland, *2 Corinthians,* New American Commentary (Nashville, TN: B & H Publishers, 1999), electronic edition.

9. William Barclay, *The Gospel of Matthew*, vol. 2, Daily Bible Study Series, second ed. (Edinburgh: Saint Andrew Press, 1964), 242.

10. Ed Hindson, "Apostasy on the Rise?" *The King Is Coming*, October 3, 2019. Accessed at https://www.thekingiscoming.com/blog/2019/10/3/apostasy-on-the-rise.

11. Mal Couch and Ed Hindson, "Apostasy," in *The Harvest Handbook of Bible Prophecy*, eds. Ed Hindson, Mark Hitchcock, Tim LaHaye (Eugene, OR: Harvest House Publishers, 2020), 45.

12. Fritz Rienecker, *A Linguistic Key to the Greek New Testament*, vol. 1 (Grand Rapids, MI: Zondervan, 1976), 198.

13. Mark Hitchcock, *Eternal Rewards* (Eugene, OR: Harvest House Publishers, 2019), 126.

14. Richard Baxter, *The Saints Everlasting Rest* (1650), (London: Epworth Press, 1962 ed.), 27.

A Final Word

1. From Ed Hindson in *The Popular Handbook on the Rapture*, eds. Tim F. LaHaye, Thomas Ice, Ed Hindson (Eugene, OR: Harvest House Publishers, 2012), 142.

Appendix: Escaping the Tribulation

1. Adapted from Ed Hindson, "Tribulation After the Rapture," *Pre-Trib Research Center*. Accessed at https://www.pre-trib.org/articles/dr-ed-hindson/message/tribulation-after-the-rapture/read.

ABOUT THE AUTHOR

Dr. Ed Hindson is the Bible teacher on *The King Is Coming* telecast and the dean emeritus of the Rawlings School of Divinity at Liberty University in Virginia, where he also serves as distinguished professor of religion. An active conference speaker and a prolific writer, Ed has written over forty books, with over three million copies in print. He also served as one of the translators of the New King James Version (NKJV) of the Bible.

He has served as the general editor of five major study Bibles, including the Gold Medallion Award-winning *Knowing Jesus Study Bible* (Zondervan) and the best-selling *King James Study Bible* (Thomas Nelson). He is coeditor of the sixteen-volume *Twenty-First Century Biblical Commentary* series on the New Testament (AMG), which includes his best-selling volume *Revelation: Unlocking the Future*.

Dr. Hindson is a graduate of William Tyndale College, holds an MA from Trinity Evangelical Divinity School and a ThM from Grace Theological Seminary, and also holds a ThD from Trinity Graduate School, a DMin from Westminster Theological Seminary, and a DLitt et Phil (PhD) from the University of South Africa. He is also a Life Fellow of the International Biographical Association (Cambridge, England).

In addition, Dr. Hindson is an adjunct professor at Veritas Evangelical University in California. He has also served as a visiting lecturer at Oxford University and the Harvard Divinity School, as well as numerous evangelical seminaries, including Dallas, Denver, Trinity, Grace, and Westminster. He has taught over 100,000 students in the past forty years, combining solid academic scholarship with a dynamic and practical teaching style.

Ed has a gift for making complicated biblical passages easy to understand for the average reader. He combines the mind of a scholar with the heart of a pastor. Ed and his wife, Donna, live in Virginia, and have three adult children and seven grandchildren. Ed says, "My greatest desire is to lift up Jesus Christ and proclaim His gospel to the entire world."

Other Great Harvest House Books
by Ed Hindson

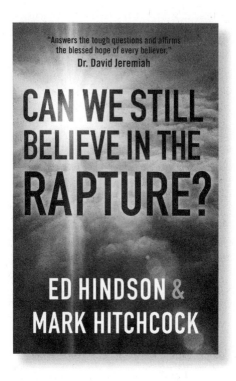

Can We Still Believe in the Rapture?
with Mark Hitchcock

Today, the hope that all believers on earth will be "caught up" to heaven is being challenged in new waves of criticism. Is the rapture really taught in the Bible? Can we really expect Jesus to gather up His followers before the Antichrist is revealed?

In this well-reasoned and thorough defense, prophecy authors Mark Hitchcock and Ed Hindson examine the concept, context, and consequences of the important and long-expected event known as the rapture. As you explore what Scripture says, you'll get a grander glimpse of your glorious future and the deepest hope of every follower of Jesus.

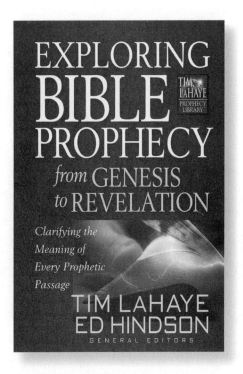

Exploring Bible Prophecy from Genesis to Revelation
with Tim LaHaye

Here is an indispensable, all-in-one resource on the prophecies of the Bible! It's all here—clear and concise explanations from Genesis to Revelation. Written by Bible scholars but created for everyday readers and Bible students, this volume makes it possible for users to expand their knowledge of Bible prophecy in ways unmatched by other books.

To learn more about Harvest House books and
to read sample chapters, visit our website:

www.harvesthousepublishers.com

HARVEST HOUSE PUBLISHERS
EUGENE, OREGON